RUNNING

Politics, Power, and the Press

By

Harry Lonsdale

© 2002 by Harry Lonsdale. All rights reserved.

No part of this book may be reproduced, stored in a retrieval system, or transmitted by any means, electronic, mechanical, photocopying, recording, or otherwise, without written permission from the author.

ISBN: 0-7596-7626-7

This book is printed on acid free paper.

1stBooks - rev. 06/15/02

In memory of
my parents

CONTENTS

Dedication iii

Foreword by The Honorable Richard D. Lamm vii

Introduction ix

Chapter 1.	Beginnings 1
Chapter 2.	Running 19
Chapter 3.	If At First You Don't Succeed… 72
Chapter 4.	…Try, Try Again 91
Chapter 5.	Fund Raising 101
Chapter 6.	The Press 118
Chapter 7.	Campaign Finance Reform And Democracy 140

Epilogue 175

Appendix A: Mark Hatfield's Fund Raising 177

Appendix B: Campaign Finance Reform And Good-Government Organizations 197

Bibliography 201

FOREWORD

There is a reverse Darwinism at work in American politics—a survival of the unfittest—as more and more good people decide not to involve themselves in politics. What thoughtful person can endure the pace, publicity, and pandering of today's politics? As in all endeavors, there are many assets and liabilities in political life, but the liabilities grow year after year. Until recently they mostly balanced out and one could face the hectic lifestyle, the media scrutiny, and the missed dinners with the family because there was a sense of civic purpose. Public policy was important and you could make a difference. Ideas did count and you could serve with integrity.

No more. With due respect to the minority of ethical and idealistic men and women who do run and serve, American politics has become an ethical wasteland. Special interest money controls. The most important factor in their election and re-election is not their ideas or integrity or principles, their platform, their talent or their thoughtfulness. But you know all this. Do you, however, realize the stakes? Many people think this is just another issue to be solved; a flaw in a system that works despite the flaw. God, after all, is an American and would never let anything happen to our great nation.

I believe this attitude is a dangerous hubris. No great nation in history has ever withstood the ravages of time. All great nations rise, then fall. Arnold Toynbee said that the "autopsy of history" is that all great nations commit suicide. Toynbee observed that those that were invaded by other nations were only overrun because they had lost the stern virtues that made them great in the first place. Could "death by suicide" be possible for this great country?

Democracy demands a certain level of virtue, integrity, and involvement from both citizens and their representatives. That virtue and integrity have been present in America but now democracy itself is in peril. With special interest contributions a candidate can purchase mindless 30-second ads today that propagandize rather than enlighten. We are in danger of becoming an economic oligarchy. In a way reminiscent of 1984, "Big Brother" money directs and controls what we think and how we choose our leaders. This is not just another issue; this is a nation-threatening issue that must be solved by the next generation of politicians.

I first ran for Governor by walking the state of Colorado. I stayed in people's homes and ate at their tables. My television spots were mostly on my walk and were all positive. I raised and spent $250,000. Today, a Colorado Governor's race costs 2 to 3 million dollars and that spending is concentrated on mindless 30-second ads on television. American political campaigns manipulate and obfuscate rather than educate. The closest correlation in winning races is how much special interest money the winner receives, nationwide.

Into this corrupting milieu in 1990 stepped a naive but dedicated, honest man. Harry Lonsdale was not a politician and didn't want to be. He was an indignant citizen who wanted to stop a variety of abuses. He had already succeeded beyond his fondest dreams. His is a wonderful American success story of a meteoric rise from poverty to great success. He knows hard work and dedication can achieve great goals, and thought this would also apply to running for political office. He sought political office for the best of reasons: because he was mad and indignant.

Harry could have retired and enjoyed his success. He did not need political office to burnish his ego. He entered politics because he was appalled by what his lovely state of Oregon was becoming. He started his political life taking on the most popular Senator in Oregon's history. It is clear that had he an even playing field, he would have won his maiden campaign. Bloody but undaunted, he continued his quest for two more brutal campaigns.

Now, he reflects on his three attempts at the U.S. Senate and what he has learned. We all profit from his lesson. This is a great story but more important it is a great warning for the nation on what U.S. politics is becoming.

This is not a Don Quixote on an impossible quest, but a hardheaded businessman on a needed crusade. He came within a few thousand votes of becoming a giant killer. His would have been a strong, needed voice in the U.S. Senate. Harry needed this office like a hole in the head, but America needed Harry to become whole. Alas, it didn't happen.

> Richard D. Lamm
> Governor of Colorado 1975-1987
> Director, Center for Public Policy
> and Contemporary Issues
> University of Denver

INTRODUCTION

This book is written for those who feel that, in spite of the current prosperity in the United States, something is wrong in our country. It is written for the majority of eligible voters—100 million of us!—who no longer even bother to vote. It is written for those who watch presidential debates on TV and wonder why neither candidate says anything of substance, and why both candidates give evasive answers to direct questions.

It is written for those who fret about all the money in political campaigns ($3 billion in the 2000 federal elections), and wonder where all that money comes from, and what it's buying.

It is written for those reluctant cynics who used to trust the Supreme Court to be above politics, used to trust the newspapers and polls, but who now find themselves in the grip of "spin-doctors" and highly paid but biased pundits, and who no longer know what to believe.

Finally, it is written for those who believe in the *idea* of America, if not its reality, who light up when they read the Declaration of Independence and celebrate the 4th of July, and who still believe in democracy and want to see our country fulfill its potential ... to put people above money, to end the corruption of money in politics, and to be a champion of peace, dignity, and justice for all people ... in short, to do the right thing.

This is a book about the game of electoral politics, as it is played at the time of the new millennium. Most of us have a love-hate relationship with things political. We hate all those pandering politicians who never give direct answers to direct questions, and we like to gloat and feel superior when they are caught in scandals of their own making. But the popularity of the whole new genre of political talk shows on prime-time TV says we're also hooked on the personalities, shenanigans, battles, and occasional heroism of the people we elect to office.

Politics has been called a "contact sport" or a game of "rough and tumble." It is that, and more. I know, first-hand. For this story came out of my own life, my several-year odyssey in an attempt to win elective office. It was a wild ride, filled with 100,000 miles behind the wheel of my car, hundreds of stump speeches, nearly 10,000 fund-raising telephone calls, and battles with members of the press who are even more cynical and thin-skinned than the rest of us. I got a glimpse—only a glimpse, really—of what the hardball game of politics is really like. And I came away from the experience convinced that until the big money is somehow taken out of elections, real democracy in our country will remain a tantalizing but frustrating dream.

Many people influenced the writing of this book, in a variety of ways. Lois Barry, Ronnie Dugger, Peter Goldman, and Roberta Kent read an early draft and made useful suggestions. Jack Ohman of The Oregonian newspaper and Wayne Stayskal of The Tampa Tribune provided me with complementary copies of their cartoons. Political cartoonists are living proof of the adage that "one picture is worth ten thousand words."

In addition, hundreds of thousands of people honored me with their votes, hundreds opened up their homes to me, thousands made campaign contributions, and hundreds of volunteers—some of the finest people I've ever known—walked with me in the rain, knocked on doors, took political risks, stuffed envelopes, wrote letters to the editor, and, most important of all, *inspired* me. For all of that and more, I am particularly indebted to Barbara Abeyta, Ric Bailey, Lois, Brian, and Jack Barry, Alan and Louisa Bateman (both deceased), Len Bergstein, former Senator Bill Bradley, Terry Bristol, Dennis Brooks, David Brower (deceased), Dannell Brown, former President Jimmy Carter, Ginny and Oscar Coen, Paul Dewey, Michael and Nina Donnelly, Chuck Duffy, Brock Evans, David Force, Jeff Golden, Debra and Bob (deceased) Grossman, Doris Haddock, John and Beth Hallett, Denis Hayes, George, Ruth, and Tim Hermach, Jim Hightower, Gary Kahn, Joe Keating, Randy Kehler, Bill and Karen Kemp, Marian and Pierre Kolisch, former Governor Dick Lamm, John Larkin, Virginia and Paul (deceased) Lemon, Tim and Karen Lillebo, Senator John McCain (even though I've never met him), Ulrich and Kathy Merten, Ralph Nader, Dana Hanson Nehl, Nancy Peterson (deceased), MaryLou and Bob Pickard, Orde Pinckney (deceased), Christy Anthony Ragan, Kris Rees, Fran Renno, Shirley Richards, Bob and Frances Riley, Jeff Rola, Russell Sadler, Peter and Debra Sage, Mitzi Scott, Dennis Stenzel, Phil Stern (deceased), Joyce Tsongas, Diane Valantine, Dani Wade, Jerry and Marilyn Wilson, Elli Work, Alex Zaffaroni, and more.

My thanks go also to Dana Hanson Nehl, Sue Walsh, and Kathy Blann who did an excellent job in typing the several drafts of the manuscript. I also want to thank Christian Kelly and his associates at First Books Library of Bloomington, Indiana, who made the book a reality.

Finally, I am indebted in more ways than I can count to my best friend, my wife, Bryn Hazell.

CHAPTER 1

BEGINNINGS

The "Pendleton Roundup" is one of the big events of the year in Oregon. Officially, it's a rodeo, and bronc busters, rodeo queens, Brahma bull riders, and calf ropers, from all over the state and from all across the country descend on this small ranching and farming community in northeast Oregon for a hell-raising week. The schools close. RVs, tents, and campers fill the parking lots and the lawns of every public space in town. The drunks and the gamblers show up, along with the ubiquitous antique auto collectors, politicians, and beauty queens.

A major part of the festivities is the parade, right through the center of town. There are floats, clowns, marching bands, the town dignitaries, the local VFW group, and all the usual trappings. The only customary thing missing from the parade are convertibles. For participants, there are only three forms of locomotion allowed: you can ride a horse, ride in a wagon, or walk.

And there I was, nervously waiting to wave to the crowd, kiss a few babies (but only if forced to), and throw some candy to the kids. Such a business! I thought to myself, is *this* the way people get elected to the U.S. Senate?!

Fortunately, a total stranger, who had heard of our Senate campaign and liked what we stood for, had offered me a ride in his wagon. I never was very much at home on a horse, and the only other alternative looked like a very long walk.

We were waiting in the holding area before the parade even got under way, when the brother of the owner of the wagon, a man about my age, rode up on his horse. I had been trained: shake every hand you can find — "if they've once shaken your hand, they'll probably vote for you." So, dutifully, I stuck out my hand to this stranger in his cowboy outfit, smiled, and repeated my mantra, "Hi, I'm Harry Lonsdale, and I'm running for the U.S. Senate." No hand was offered in return. I couldn't recall anyone ever refusing my handshake ... even people who didn't like me would shake my hand. And I've done the same.

So I reached farther out of the wagon, almost touching him. He backed his horse up, to avoid me. Undaunted, I jumped out of the wagon, pursued him, and again extended my hand. No deal.

Exasperated, I asked him, "Why won't you shake my hand, sir?"

His caustic reply, "What do *you* want to go back to Washington and steal?"

That was all; he rode off. I shouted after him, "But *I* want to go back there and clean it up!" but to no avail. If he heard me, he showed no recognition. I was shouting into the wind. His mind was made up: all politicians were crooks.

Welcome to the world of politics, Harry.

# # #

It's only a short hop by commuter plane from Roberts Field in Redmond, Oregon to Portland International Airport. Even in the small turboprops that United Airlines and Alaska Airlines use to provide air service to and from central Oregon, the flight-time is only about 40 minutes. Barely enough time to settle into your seat, scan the airline magazine, and take a short nap.

But on a clear day it's one of the more spectacular flights in the country. Frequently, you fly almost directly over 10,500-foot Mt. Jefferson, and 11,300-foot Mt. Hood, the highest mountain in Oregon, is just north of the flight path. Mt. Adams, Mt. St. Helens, and the Three Sisters mountains are all clearly visible. From the cruise altitude of about 15,000 feet, it seems you could almost reach out and touch those magnificent snow-capped, dormant volcanoes of the Cascade Range.

By the mid-1980s, I had lived in my adopted home of Bend, Oregon a dozen years or so, and my business trips had taken me on that familiar Redmond-Portland flight a hundred times or more. I had moved to Oregon from California in 1972 because of what I felt was the unmatched quality of life of the Pacific Northwest. My earliest business and vacation travels had taken me to almost every state in the U.S. and to a number of foreign countries. Oregon impressed me as the best of the best. It had everything ... mountains, rivers, forests, the ocean, wildlife, deserts, clean air and water, an equitable climate, and, best of all, almost no people, compared with California.

What I hadn't realized until I had lived there for a while was that the timber industry was the state's largest employer, and that what kept that industry alive was clear-cutting those magnificent stands of towering Douglas fir, ponderosa pine, and other varieties of trees that made some of the best lumber in the world.

And so, on one of those Redmond-Portland flights, I finally saw what I had been missing for years. Clearly delineated by winter snows were miles and miles of clearcuts. Most of those forests that made Oregon uniquely Oregon were gone. And what was left would surely be gone soon. And then what?

# # #

I began to ask a few questions. Who owned those forests? Who controlled them? How much was left? What would happen when it was all gone ... to the economy? ... to the environment? ... to Oregon? I took my questions to the local headquarters of the U. S. Forest Service, only to learn that they didn't have any satisfying answers. They saw their job mainly as "getting out the timber cut."

For me, the problem became acute when it reached the Metolius. The most beautiful place I know of on this planet is the Metolius River, near a little town named Sisters in central Oregon. The river is spring-fed, ice-cold, and gin-clear, year 'round. I learned that the Forest Service was planning a timber sale *directly along* the river, essentially destroying that pristine spot. The USFS staff held hearings in Sisters, inviting the locals to comment on the sale. In the end, after months of squabbling, the timber sale was canceled and the Metolius was spared (so far). But that was only my initiation.

The dominant, observable use of our forests is for timber production. The federal laws that established the national forests at the beginning of the 20th century, and that provide for their management even today, call for those forests to be managed on a "sustained-yield" basis. To most of us, "sustained yield" means that whatever we extract from the forests as timber, we allow the forests to grow back, over time. The reality, sadly, is vastly different. Of the original virgin forests that covered most of what is now the U.S. when the Jamestown settlers arrived from England 400 years ago, 95% or more is gone. And even the national forests, which belong to all of us, have been decimated. How much is left is the subject of considerable debate, but estimates range down to as low as 2% of the native forests. Converting those forests to lumber is one of our country's oldest industries. Timber towns are sprinkled all across the Western landscape. Many of them go back to the 19th century, and some of those towns boast of 3rd and 4th generation loggers. For many of those small, rural towns, timber production is the *only* industry, and is the basis of their entire economy. It is a way of life for thousands of good people who work in the woods.

But something is very wrong in the way the forests on our public lands have been managed. Most of the older trees have been cut down, and many of those forests have been converted into tree farms. It is easy to be fooled about the condition of our forests if you just look at the green areas on maps, or if you stick to the highways. The true nature of things isn't revealed until you walk back into the woods a mere quarter mile from the highway or, better yet, drive on any of the hundreds of thousands of miles of U. S. Forest Service roads that honeycomb our forests. The most revealing of all is the view from an airplane, where "moonscapes" are revealed all across the Western states. Federal regulations require that all of the logged-over lands must be replanted with seedlings, and many of them have been. But with shrinking USFS budgets over the years, the replanting program is one of the first to be cut back.

It isn't just that much of the forest resource is gone, probably forever, it is the way in which our forests have been "harvested" that anyone except a logger or a professional forester would find repugnant. Our forests are routinely clear-cut. That is, every tree, whether or not it has commercial value, is cut down, and the non-valuable trees and the branches—know as "slash"—are piled up and burned. Then, the area is sprayed with herbicide to prevent the growth of non-commercial species, and the area is replanted with a monoculture of seedlings, if it is replanted at all. And then, every 40 or 50 years, the area is clear-cut again. This process has been on-going in some of the forests in the wet Pacific Northwest for up to 100 years, or three cycles. It is not yet clear if the cycle can be repeated indefinitely. Trees, like all plants, need nutrients from the soil, both inorganic and biological, and these nutrients are lost as the timber is hauled away, as the slash is burned, and as the exposed soils are washed away in rainstorms.

*Running
Politics, Power, and the Press*

**Winter snows highlight clearcuts in the Mt. Hood National Forest, Oregon.
Photo ©Timothy Hermach.**

Monocultural tree farms are not forests. And clearcuts are ugly beyond words. When an area has been clear-cut, most of the essential values except timber production have been lost.

# # #

For many years, a tension had been growing between the timber industry and environmentalists all across the West. Things really heated up in the early '80s, when interest rates on home mortgages went through the roof, and new-home construction—perforce tied closely to interest rates—hit its lowest level in decades. Timber production fell precipitously, many mills were shut down, and loggers and mill workers lost their jobs. On the environmentalist side, awareness was increasing that our forests had been drastically overcut for decades, there wasn't much of the ancient forest left—almost none on private lands—and new environmental groups sprang up all across the country, while the established groups, like the Sierra Club and the Wilderness Society, grew in strength and influence.

Some timber-dependent communities literally disappear. Others hang on, but remain poor. But still others, like my hometown of Bend, Oregon, adapt. In the early '80s, Bend was a blue-collar, one-industry town. At one time, 1250 people, out of a town population of 12,000, worked at the mill. At the bottom of the early '80s recession, local unemployment hit 14%, and fully a third of all the downtown stores were closed. Within a decade, however, the mill was completely shut down, unemployment was at 6%, and the economy was booming: new shopping centers went up, and the town population doubled and then doubled again. What happened was that the people who had made money in the timber-dependent days stayed and invested, and new entrepreneurs, attracted by the climate, the open spaces, and the quality of life, came to town and created new industries: high tech, tourism, secondary wood products, services, light industry, Internet companies, and more.

Many of the poor Western towns remain trapped in the past. High school kids drop out to take a high paying job at the mill. Ten dollars an hour to start looks a lot more attractive than studying algebra. But, when the downturn comes, their limited skills become worthless. There are layoffs at the mill and – if the mill owner resides some place far away, as many of them do – it's pretty easy to just shut the mill down. The high school graduate, now making $20 an hour, with a nice pick-up truck, married with a couple of kids, and living in a double-wide trailer, can no longer afford the payments on his possessions. Options are limited. Twenty dollars an hour looks great to someone with a limited education and narrowly defined skills. But how many hours do they work per year? What happens when the unemployment checks run out? Our laissez-faire, devil-take-the-hindmost economy can be especially harsh on the folks working in natural-resource extraction.

# # #

My life began to change one day in the mid-'80s when I drove to Eugene, Oregon for a breakfast meeting with a man named George Hermach. George was recently retired, an avid outdoorsperson, along with his family, and he was encyclopedic about our forests. Eugene sits on the edge of the Willamette National Forest, the most productive of all of our national forests, in terms of timber production. Eugene and the smaller communities around it are highly dependent on timber for their economy. Only the presence of the University of Oregon and some budding high tech industry keeps Eugene from being one more timber town. And George was as attached to "his" Willamette National Forest as I was to "my" Metolius. George gave me a real education that day. I learned that, while in principle the national forests are public land and are therefore owned by We The People, in practice they are controlled by the U.S. Congress through the U.S. Forest Service. Each year, Congress sets a timber cut level and the USFS complies by putting federal timber up for sale to the timber companies. The timber company owners and their lobbyists are well connected politically and for years they have gotten the USFS to sell off our forest lands at well beyond sustainable levels. We taxpayers paid to build the logging roads so that the timber companies could get to the trees, while the timber companies sold some of the timber overseas as raw logs, thereby putting some of their own millworkers out of work.

Our forests were disappearing, "sustainability" was a farce, jobs were being lost, and most of the public was unaware of it all. It was a real revelation to me and it smelled bad. I started going to conferences put on by environmentalists and forests activists, folks known locally as "tree-huggers". In meetings all across Oregon and as far away as Texas and Washington, D.C., I met some of the finest and most dedicated people I've ever known.

At about the same time, things got tight in the Oregon timber industry, for several reasons. First, the industry began to modernize, eliminating thousands of jobs to automation. Second, new housing starts were down all across the country, reducing the demand for wood products. And finally, environmentalists had achieved some success in curtailing timber sales through legal challenges involving the Endangered Species Act. In that tight job market, it wasn't difficult for the mill owners to motivate their employees to action. The timber industry's public relations people created the "Yellow Ribbon Coalition" all across rural Oregon to organize workers and their families to demonstrate actively for increased timber production from public lands. Photos of mothers holding their purportedly hungry babies filled the newspapers and TV screens. A small but vocal lobbying group called the Wise Use

Movement originated in Seattle, calling for increased use of public lands for ranching and mining, as well as increased timber production all across the West, and a loosening of environmental laws. On occasion, hundreds of log trucks circled our state capitol in Salem, honking their horns in protest. Employers stuffed notices into their employee's paychecks, telling them to write to their Congressperson and their Senators to get them to pass laws to increase timber sales on public lands. In many cases, postcards were already printed and stamped, requiring only the employee's signature before being mailed to Washington, D.C. Videos, from 30-second "spots" to longer format pieces, featuring unemployed loggers with their families, were distributed around the state in an expensive and effective public-relations campaign.

The industry slogan was "Trees are America's renewable resource. We cut them down to build houses out of, but they grow back." But the industry had no intention—nor did the Forest Service—of replacing the 500-year-old trees, or the forests, that they were taking.

The argument escalated and nasty words turned into nastier deeds. Earth First(!)ers came out of the woodwork, and "monkey-wrenching" began. People chained themselves to trees. Sit-ins began in USFS offices, frequently resulting in arrests. Trees were spiked, in order to ruin the giant bandsaws in the mills, first with steel spikes and later, to avoid detection by metal detectors, with concrete spikes. The timber companies hired private cops to protect their private lands and to prevent environmentalists from camping high up in trees about to be logged on public lands. Tree-huggers were arrested for entering the forests, first in ones and twos, later in dozens, scores, and even hundreds. Bumper stickers from both sides of the issue appeared on cars owned by people who had never been involved in any movement. Newspaper editorials and letters to the editor were filled with invective. A non-shooting war had broken out, the wounds from which are still with us today.

The war escalated further when the spotted owl entered the picture. Back in 1973, Congress passed the Endangered Species Act, one of the most important and far-reaching pieces of legislation ever enacted. In essence, it said that We The People through our elected representatives will not knowingly allow any species to go extinct because of human activities.

By the mid-1980s a wildlife biologist found that the Northern Spotted Owl, which lived almost exclusively in the ancient forests of the Pacific

Northwest, was in danger of going extinct because of the loss of its habitat. After more research and much debate, the spotted owl was listed as an endangered species by the U.S. Fish and Wildlife Service. One could properly conclude that that meant its habitat would thereafter be protected. What happened, instead, was a string of lawsuits originated by both the environmental community and the timber industry. What was at stake was the disposition of millions of acres of forests which, when reduced to timber, were worth many billions of dollars.

The timber industry and their friends in Congress made short work of the lawsuit problem. In 1989 Congress passed a rider to the 1989 federal budget stipulating that timber sales on certain public lands would be made in spite of any and all environmental laws. In addition to the Endangered Species Act, other laws were on the books defining in general terms how the forests on public lands would be managed, such as the National Forest Management Act and the National Environmental Policy Act.

The rider, which became known among tree-huggers as the "Rider from Hell", contained this language: "Notwithstanding any other provision in law ... [timber sales will proceed]" What Congress was saying with this language was, essentially, "We made all those earlier environmental laws and, anytime we want to, we can unmake them." And they did. But it wasn't without consequence. Logging protests went through the roof. Hundreds of people, some of them grandmothers this time, went to jail. The war was engaged in earnest from both sides. The national media became involved. And both sides quickly learned how to "work" the media.

# # #

At about that time, mid-1989, I happened to be on a short field-trip to survey a proposed timber sale near the headwaters of spring-fed Jack Creek, a tributary of my beloved Metolius River. With me were Tim Lillebo, a biologist working for Oregon's most important environmental group, the Oregon Natural Resources Council; Larry Tuttle, a banker-turned-environmentalist who had served as one of our county commissioners; and Norm Johnson, a forestry professor at Oregon State University and the governor's chief forestry advisor. Except for Johnson, we were all tree-huggers, and so the conversation that day turned naturally to the rape of the forests. Lillebo and Tuttle were well ahead of me in understanding that the problem lay not just with the timber company owners and managers. Nor did the problem reside exclusively with the Forest Service, although we didn't respect them as a group, for not standing up to Congress when they knew damn well that congressional mandates were forcing them to overcut the forests. My friends knew that the problem rested squarely with Congress itself. That knowledge was what had led Tuttle to run twice against our representative in the U. S. Congress, Bob Smith—although Tuttle never came close to winning.

Offhandedly, I made the wild proposal that *I* run against Smith in the next election. "No, not Smith", said Tuttle. "If you're going to run, run against Neil Goldschmidt or Mark Hatfield." Goldschmidt at the time was our governor and a fellow Democrat, and I rather liked him. His forest policy was bad, but the big forests in Oregon aren't under the control of the governor or even our state legislature. They are the national forests, controlled by the USFS and, ultimately, by Congress.

As for U. S. Senator Mark Hatfield, it seemed he had been in office since the pyramids were built. He first won elected office when he was in his late 20s, and had served in the Oregon House and the Oregon Senate, as Oregon's Secretary of State (our lieutenant governor's title), as governor for two terms, and for four terms as our U.S. Senator. He'd never lost an election. He was the darling of the Oregon press. He had been described as the most "undefeatable politician in Oregon history". And, while he was a Republican and I leaned Democrat, he was considered a moderate on most issues. Even his rotten forest policy was considered by the press a good compromise between the environment and the economy.

What he was best known for, and admired for among many Oregonians (including me, at the time), was his strong anti-war position. As a result, he became known among his many admirers in the press as a man of principle.

Me, run against *him*? Preposterous!

Still, I rolled it around in my mind for a few weeks.

One day, I was driving across the Cascade Mountains with my friend Bill Marlett to attend an environmental conference in the Willamette Valley. Bill is one of those strong-willed but soft-spoken men who lets his actions speak for him. He has an excellent academic background in ecology and the environment, and he could probably earn a multiple of his salary if he went to work for some establishment firm. Instead, he worked for peanuts, starting local environmental organizations, ultimately even helping to create an environmental center in Bend. I once asked Bill why he did what he did. He answered in his usual simple but clear way, "It's the most important thing to do."

Bill and I talked on that long car trip about the forests, and about the possibility of my challenging Mark Hatfield for his Senate seat the next year. Bill's typically short but all-encompassing statement was, "What do you have to do that's more important?"

"Well, nothing, when you put it that way. But there's no chance I could win."

"How do you know? And besides, even if you lose, you'll expose his stupid timber policy and maybe get him to change it."

I thought on it. And thought on it. For a time, I couldn't get it out of my mind. A Senator *does* have a lot of clout. One Senator can bring things to a halt with a filibuster. And even the threat of a filibuster is a powerful weapon. And, while a freshman Senator doesn't have much influence, after a few years ...

But I'm too much a victim of my own principles, I told myself, to ever fit into the Senate. I'm too much black-and-white, too uncompromising on the things I believe in. I'd quickly become marginalized in the Senate as someone who won't play ball.

My friend Tim Lillebo had some good advice on that problem. He had lobbied members of Congress for years and was pretty familiar with how the system works. His advice: there are some things you believe in, no matter what, and you will not compromise on those. Then there are things you care about but that aren't gut issues with you. And then there are all the other issues that you don't know about and don't care much about. Get what you want, and, when possible, give them what they want. It sounded to me like just the way the system works, and it was just that "you scratch my back and I'll scratch yours" system that I disliked. Maybe, if I got there, I could hold my nose ...

# # #

Slowly, I began to take stock. Eventually, when I got serious, I began to write some thoughts down. Just what *were* my credentials? For starters, I came from strong stock. My father was orphaned in New Jersey when he was two years old, literally left on a doorstep. He only finished the fourth grade in school and yet, through determination and hard work, he and my mom had realized a small piece of the American dream.

My mother was born in a tiny village in Sicily. Her parents left home for America when she was only 9 months old. She traveled down to the sea to emigrate to the United States in her mother's arms on the back of a donkey. They settled in New Jersey, where my mom only finished the eighth grade.

There's no way — short of another entire book — to describe growing up during the Depression of the '30s, as I did, when 30% of working people were unemployed. Life was a scramble for my uneducated parents, culminating in our family-owned chicken and egg farm, where I was raised.

My parents tried to teach me the important values: hard work, tenacity, honesty, loyalty, finishing what you start, humility, and more. I wish I could claim that I learned all that they taught.

I had the benefit of a good education. I entered Rutgers, the state university of New Jersey, on an academic scholarship and, inspired by my high school science teacher, I majored in chemistry (*anything* but chickens!). I then went on to earn a Ph.D. in chemistry from Penn State.

After college, I married my high school sweetheart and we started a family. I spent two years as a lieutenant in the United States Air Force, fulfilling an ROTC commitment. It allowed me to see most of the United States, if only superficially. I then spent the next dozen years as a scientific researcher in private industry in California, eventually reaching a middle management position.

In the early '70s, bored with life as an employee in an industrial research setting, I quit my job in California, moved to Bend, Oregon with my family, spent a year as a visiting scientist in research laboratories in Germany and Israel, and returned to Oregon to start a high tech company with a former scientific colleague. We named our company Bend Research, Inc. after our new hometown. Our "business" was selling research, within our area of expertise, to anyone who wanted to buy it, government agencies or private companies, foreign or domestic.

In assessing my qualifications to hold an important public office, I counted heavily on my business background. Most of the members of

Congress are lawyers by training, although many of them never actually practiced law in any serious way. Very few members had ever met a payroll, or knew how to prepare, let alone balance, a budget ... and it showed in our national debt. By the late 1980s, I had traveled to some three dozen countries, primarily on business trips, and I had lived outside of the U.S. for a year. My travels had exposed me to other cultures, and other ways of seeing things. Our country, it seemed to me, had some things to learn from other societies in the areas of taxation, gun control, universal healthcare, crime prevention through job creation, and even in how we make laws. Those were some ideas and values I'd be delighted to take to the U.S. Senate.

As for my qualifications, I had served as chair of a couple of Governor's commissions, but I'd never joined the typical service clubs or chamber of commerce that business people frequently join. Nor had I ever run for political office.

Probably my most significant civic achievement was the creation of what we called the Great Oregon Spring Cleanup. It was a springtime roadside litter cleanup campaign. For years, while taking my daily walk, I would pick up litter by the side of the road. One day, I posted on the company bulletin board a notice that I was going to pick up litter along the roads near where we worked. Anyone willing to join me would be given time off from work, and I would buy them a fast-food lunch when we were done picking up litter. Fifteen people showed up that first year. Two years later we invited the townspeople to join us, with the help of some radio and newspaper public service announcements; 160 people came. The following year, 600; then 1100; and finally we hit a peak of 2000 people, including about 1000 school kids. That year, and subsequent years, we picked up litter along 200 miles of roads, and collected about 4000 bags of trash. It became an annual Bend event.

I had one other asset in running for office, probably more important than all the others combined. In the course of our work at Bend Research, we had invented a technology that a major U.S. pharmaceutical company wanted to buy. By the time the negotiations were over, they had bought a piece of our company, and I had personally pocketed more than a million dollars. Money had never meant much to me. But it gave me the freedom to do, within reason, whatever I wanted to do with the rest of my life, even the freedom of running for office.

Along with my assets in running for office, I also had some significant liabilities. At the top of the list, I had never held any public office, had never even run for public office, and I was almost totally unknown to the voters of Oregon. Most people in public office start on their career of public service early in their lives. They run for school board or the water commission or county commission, then maybe for the state legislature, and so on, each step along the way building a group of supporters and increasing their name recognition to the voters. But if a poll had been taken in 1989 to determine *my* name identification in Oregon, it might have shown that less than 1% of Oregonians knew my name. So, there was liability No. 1, and a big one: zero name-I.D.

There was more. I was shy (although my close friends might not think so; in small groups, I could be very outspoken, could hog the conversation). I hated crowds, and still do. At parties, I was a wallflower, usually attempting to find one person with whom I could carry on an intelligent conversation. I had never starred in a high school play, had never taken speech or debate in high school or college, and had given very few speeches except for scientific talks. Like most people, I had a great fear of public speaking, and tended to get "dry mouth" when I forced myself to do it. I came to understand why so many successful politicians had once been seminarians, or successful trial lawyers, or actors. Some people, it surprised me to learn, actually *enjoyed* getting up in front of a group and speaking, even extemporaneously.

To add to the list, I wasn't connected to the Oregon business or social establishment. And I would need establishment support in my campaign.

Even the prospect of leaving Oregon and moving to Washington, D.C., in the event that I should win, didn't hold much appeal. And some of the members of Congress themselves, having been the victims of hatchet jobs in the press, and of their own misdeeds, didn't seem like a bunch I wanted to work with.

Finally, by the late 1980s, I was a divorced person. Divorce was no longer the stigma it once had been. But it meant that I was alone with no No. 1 confidante with whom to share my dreams and fears. I had a good circle of close friends, but it's not the same as a soul-mate.

So that was it: some plusses, some minuses.

# # #

What makes people run for public office? There are probably as many reasons as there are candidates.

Some simply want power. Some are genuinely interested in public service. Others want the spotlight. For a few, it's a single, dominant issue: war-and-peace, the environment, women's rights, whatever. Rarely is money the prime motivator. Initially, at least, I was a one-issue candidate: I wanted to save what was left of the forests on public lands.

I vacillated for many weeks. This was no small decision. It meant taking a leave of absence from my job, a job I adored, and, if successful, leaving it entirely. It meant heading down a road I'd never been on before, with a totally uncertain result, and with many surprises, fears, frustrations, and lessons along the way.

What made the decision particularly wrenching was the reaction I got from my closest friends. When I tried the idea out on them, most wouldn't even look me in the eye. "You're gonna get beat," they'd say, "and it will hurt." My reaction to that was to talk more with people who encouraged me.

At one point, I was ready to go. The next day, I wasn't so sure. The following day I said, "No way." Then the pull came back again. On and off, on and off. Even my old and trusted method of reaching tough decisions wasn't working. I made columns of pros and cons, even weighting the various factors and then adding them up to reach a final score. It didn't work. If I reached a decision that I wasn't comfortable with that day, I changed the weighting, to make it come out the way I wanted it to (that day). Finally, I made a pact with myself: if I felt the same way, either way—up or down—3 days in a row, I'd live by that decision.

Slowly, I came to realize that serving in Congress wasn't just about saving the forests or even an important national issue like campaign finance reform. It was about being a part of running the entire country! True, a member of Congress is only one vote, and even the President doesn't get his way much of the time. But, still, there were many issues facing America. I ran them through my mind, and tried to find my own position on them. Foreign policy? I knew that much of the world looked to us for leadership. But I also knew that many people, even in the democracies, thought of us as a bully, pushing countries around, even invading a few, especially in the "American hemisphere". We also were the world's largest arms exporter. If I had my druthers, I'd stop exporting *all* arms and arm-wrestle with our trading partners to do the same. Our primary export, it seemed to me, should be *democracy*.

The military? Having served in it myself, I felt that it was not just bloated and inefficient, it was simply *too big*. The U.S. shouldn't be the world's policeman. Leave that job to a strong U.N. No "Star Wars". No more B-2 bombers. The Cold War was over.

The budget and the national debt? In my company, we never borrowed money unless we absolutely had to. And just about every successful business was run that way. Interest paid on the debt could drag down a country just as surely as it could drag down a company, it seemed to me. It was just too easy for Congress to give money away in a thousand different ways — welfare, "pork", aircraft carrier fleets, social security, Medicare, and all the rest — and too difficult for those gutless poll-watchers to ask the people to pay for it all. I felt that we should create new, family-wage jobs to put more people on the tax rolls. End corporate welfare, in all of its forms. The Republicans in Congress liked to talk about class warfare and all the selfishness and envy that implies. But, if we had class warfare in this country, it was because the rich were getting richer while the poor were left behind. Corporate execs. were making a million dollars a year and more. The minimum wage was $4 an hour. Where was the *fairness*?

Social Security and Medicare? These are the two largest budgetary outlays of our government, and, according to then-current projections, the income would soon be less than the outgo. The answer didn't seem too complex to me: either raise more money, by increasing the FICA tax for everyone, or, preferably, on those most able to pay, that is, remove the cap on FICA deductions; or pay out less money, especially to those who didn't need it. The latter approach was called "means testing", which seemed straightforward and fair to me.

Healthcare? I felt that everyone should have affordable health coverage throughout their lives, just as they did in every other industrialized country, and just as we provided for seniors in our own country.

Tobacco? Shut the industry down and stop addicting and killing people — 400,000 a year in the U.S., millions worldwide.

TV? Clean it up. There had to be a way to encourage the industry to police itself.

Welfare, drugs, and crime? Create living-wage jobs, even if the government had to create them, as it did during the Great Depression. Better yet, create incentives for private industry.

Working people, job security, foreign competition? A particular thorn in my side was the imbalance of power between labor and management. Labor unions had been pretty well dismembered in our country by means of a single inequity: striking workers could be legally and permanently replaced with non-union labor. The right to strike had become the right to quit!

The environment? Sustainability had to be our goal. What can we do, and how can we live our lives, so that 1000 years from now people can enjoy at least as good a standard of living as we're enjoying today? As one small step, we could repeal the 1872 Mining Law that allows mining companies to extract minerals and then *buy the land* for $2.50 an acre! We should make trees truly "America's renewable resource", and a lot more.

And what about our "public airwaves"? Surely, the best way to inform the public, expose campaign finance corruption, fight prejudice and bigotry, improve citizenship and reduce cynicism, and, in general, to "make a more perfect union," is through television. But television in the U.S., more than in any other country that I have visited, is a business, run by people who want to show a profit to their shareholders. Most programming is aimed at holding our attention so that advertisers can sell us their products. I felt that we needed a major shift toward truly publicly owned-and-operated TV networks.

# # #

When our country was founded in 1787, an elite few made all of the major decisions: how the Constitution was worded, who got elected, etc. Decisions, at least all the important ones, are still being made by a handful of people in Washington, D.C., and they still represent, in many cases, the will of a small minority. Members of Congress don't listen to We The People much. Oh, their office doors are always open, and they help locate that lost Social Security check and perform other minor acts of constituent service, but when it comes down to the big issues – tobacco, taxes, gun control, the military, poverty, corporate power, and more, the "big boys" and their highly paid lobbyists are still running the show ... and pulling the wool over our eyes. The people who have the ear of

Congress, the people who, in some cases, actually sit at the elbow of Congressmen and help write legislation that affects all of us, are the people who write the big campaign-contribution checks.

# # #

America may be the greatest country in the world, but it still needed a lot of fixing. And what was I going to try to do about it? My big issue was still saving our national forests, but I realized that to achieve that I'd really have to tackle a much larger issue: campaign finance reform.

What I really wanted was a *voice*. Some members of Congress and, especially, Senators have a national voice. That thought was probably what put me over the top. Saving the forests and campaign finance reform, my two top issues, couldn't be achieved by any one person, no matter how well intentioned or highly motivated, unless that person had (or could purchase) a national voice.

To achieve what I felt driven to achieve meant running for Congress and winning a seat there. But running against whom? There was my Congressman, Bob Smith of Oregon's vast Second Congressional District — it covers an area of 60,000 square miles. Bob was a "good ole boy", a conservative Republican, quite a likable man even if wrong on most of the issues I cared about, and virtually undefeatable. He'd been in office for five terms and had never been seriously challenged. But he wasn't my target. He had little control over our national forests. Besides, House members had to run for re-election every two years — a noxious job that I'd just as soon avoid.

Bob Packwood, our junior Senator? My beef wasn't with him, even though he was certainly more vulnerable to defeat than Hatfield.

No, it had to be Hatfield, "Mr. Invulnerable." He alone led the attack on our forests, including pushing the outrageous "Rider from Hell" through the Senate. And he represented all the ills of long-term incumbency I'd come to despise, a pork-barreler who worked the system well.

At one point, in late '89, the soul-searching finally ended. I knew that I could do a good job in the Senate if only I could get there.

CHAPTER 2.

RUNNING

Having finally made my mind up to do it, and having picked my opponent, all that was left was figuring out how to *win*.

I started out with a set of principles, a strong desire to change some things in Washington, D.C., some money in the bank, and not much else. Where to begin?

I had read somewhere that election campaigns usually have a campaign manager to "run things," whatever that meant. I didn't know any professional campaign managers, of course—there are only a handful of them in all of Oregon. But I did have a friend in Portland, Terry Bristol, who was considerably better connected with the establishment than I was. He was bright, energetic, shared my entrepreneurial spirit, and had a science background. At that time, Terry and his wife were in the early stages of putting together a science lecture series in Oregon. Ultimately, it was to become a huge success, attracting people like Carl Sagan, Jane Goodall, and others to huge and appreciative audiences in Portland and Eugene.

When I told Terry that I was running and what I believed in, and then offered him the job of campaign manager, he dropped his other activities and accepted. It was my first exposure to one of the positive aspects of running for public office: noble people, inspired by patriotism and the still unfulfilled dream of real democracy, seem to appear out of nowhere and offer to help, even at considerable personal sacrifice.

And then came another break: Kris Rees offered to join our team. Kris was an old friend from Bend. She and I had dated a few times, although nothing serious ever came of it. But we had gotten to know one another well. Kris was vivacious, self-assured, intelligent, hard working, and politically active, if on a local scale. At the time, she had an excellent job with a local land developer in Bend, selling real estate. She was also a life-long Republican, hailing from a tiny wheat-farming community in northeastern Oregon. But when I told her I was running, she offered to quit her job and sign on as "finance director," meaning chief fund-raiser. Here was another principled person willing to take a risk. What I found most surprising was that my set of core principles appealed to a die-hard Republican. My business background had a lot to do with it, and Kris believed as strongly as I did that Washington, D.C. was a mess that needed cleaning up. And she believed that I was just stubborn enough and determined enough to go and do something about it.

We had the beginnings of our campaign team.

We then heard about a three-day Senate candidates' school that the Democratic Party put on during election years, outside of Washington, D.C. Kris and I went. Talk about plunging into the deep end of the pool! Perhaps half of the Democrats who were thinking seriously about running for the U.S. Senate that year were there. Some were there for the second time. Almost all of them had some political experience. They had either run for office before or, more likely, they held elected office at some lower level. The point is, they knew the ropes; I didn't. Among other attendees was Harvey Gantt, the mayor of Charlotte, NC, who was planning to challenge Jesse Helms. That made him an immediate hero to me.

We were given a 4"-thick, 3-ring notebook jam-packed with advice, lists, consultants, Democratic principles, financial data, and more. "Here, take this notebook home tonight and study it..."

We received instructions from some of the finest pros in the business. And, yes, I realized, it *is* a business, a big business. And those at the top of the list make a pretty good living at it.

There were parallel sessions, and Kris attended one while I attended another. We attempted to compare notes at the end of the day but I was too exhausted and overwhelmed with information to be worth much at the end of the day. We watched videos produced by the Democratic Senatorial Campaign Committee (DSCC) featuring prominent Senators urging us on—people like John Breaux of Louisiana, who was then head of the DSCC, majority leader George Mitchell, and Joe Lieberman of Connecticut.

We picked up two important pieces of information from the candidates' school. First—actually, it's first, second, and third—we learned the importance of money in modern political campaigns. "Modern" here means "television-based", which all successful statewide and federal campaigns are these days. Money. If you didn't have it, get it. If you can't get it, don't bother to run—or at least don't expect to win. We heard stories about how much money successful candidates, and especially incumbents, raised and spent on their Senate campaigns. Even challengers, at least the serious ones, were raising and spending a million dollars or more.

You hear "a million dollars" and it simply doesn't register. Just how much money *is* that? And where does it come form? And what does it take to bring it in? *Spending* it seemed easy; it was the raising part that looked difficult and mysterious. (And, it would turn out, very time-consuming.) Yes, I had some money of my own. But was it enough? And, if not, where was I to raise more?

The second useful bit of information we brought home with us was a list of political consultants. These were people who worked on campaigns in a variety of capacities: campaign managers, fund-raisers, media consultants (who produced those deadly little 30-second "spots" that we see on TV), pollsters, even organizations that ran phone banks or printed bumper stickers, or who did "opposition research". The latter, I learned, combined the talents of private investigators with those of researchers who dug up dirt on your opponent, for pay. Those folks will even dig up dirt on *you*, their client, so that you will know in advance what dirt your opponent is digging up on you, so that you can prepare your defense. "Is this what it's all about?" I asked myself.

I also realized, from that 3-day school, that I was entering another world, totally foreign to me. And it didn't look pretty.

One of the more pleasant parts of my dealing with the DSCC was meeting several Democratic Senators: Bill Bradley, John Breaux, Richard Bryan, Al Gore, Joe Lieberman, Howard Metzenbaum, George Mitchell, Sam Nunn, and Jay Rockefeller. Nice men, all of them: friendly, down-to-earth, easy to meet and converse with, intelligent, patriotic Americans. The sort of people you'd love to have dinner with and compare life experiences with. I thought, "It would be fun to work with these guys." But still, I wondered, don't these guys raise millions for their re-election campaigns? How do they do that? Does anyone own them, or any part of them?

Back home in Oregon, I rented an apartment in Portland to be closer to the political action. The trouble was, there wasn't any action. I didn't know how an election campaign was supposed to proceed, but I suspected it was made up of large doses of meeting people, giving speeches, and, most importantly, getting your name and your positions in front of the voters through the media. I didn't know how to make that happen, and neither did my campaign manager. With some misgivings, I decided to turn to the professionals back in Washington, D.C.

The DSCC supplied me with a list of names from their job bank, and I interviewed a few people with some experience in managing congressional campaigns. I felt that one person was clearly superior to the others. I offered her the job, and she accepted.

She was Karen Olick, a native of New York City, who had worked in the successful U.S. Senate campaign of Frank Lautenberg of New Jersey in 1988, where she learned the ropes from James Carville—before Carville became famous by masterminding Bill Clinton's 1992 Presidential campaign.

Like most Easterners, Karen didn't know beans about Oregon. She mispronounced Ory-gone and Willa-*mette* the way they all do (and as I once did). But she more than made up for those minor flaws with her intelligence, drive, determination, guts, daring, and experience. Over the next few months, I came to respect her greatly, and I still do.

Exit my friend Terry Bristol, to go back to doing what he did best: run a science-lecture series. Enter Karen Olick. The business of politics had begun.

# # #

For the amateur, it's hard to imagine what goes into a bona fide U.S. Senate campaign, especially for a political unknown like me. Karen knew. She knew that people didn't vote for you—except for those few who did so to vote *against* your opponent —unless they (a) knew your name, (b) knew at least something about you, and (c) preferred your positions on one or two key issues to those of your opponent.

Before she accepted the job, Karen had given *me* the third degree. Any arrests? (No) Any messy divorces? (Two, but neither was messy). Any embarrassing public statements? (None that I could think of). Drinker? (No). Philanderer? (No). Ever been sued? (No). ANY SCANDALS OF ANY SORT? (*NO*). Why are you running? My answers seemed to satisfy her. To a real pro in this business, they probably seemed corny and idealistic. She seemed to find them refreshing. How much of your own money are you prepared to spend on this race? (Dunno. How does $300,000 sound? $500,000 tops.)

Now Karen must have known, even though I didn't, that even $500,000 wasn't nearly enough dough to defeat a long-term, generally well liked incumbent like Hatfield. But she let me learn the money lesson for myself, the hard way.

Karen signed on in early February 1990. The primary election was less than 5 months away. Within a month, we had rented an office in downtown Portland, complete with half a dozen phone lines, in a great location: directly across the street from the main county library. And we had put together the beginnings of a great staff. Dan Walter, who had experience with CBS and The New York Times, came on as the press secretary. Carrie Goux became my scheduler, a very demanding and important job. Christy Anthony, a Portland native who was also a sharp, young Democratic activist who had worked on the Dukakis for President campaign, became our volunteer coordinator. Gary Kahn, an environmentalist-lawyer buddy, agreed to handle our legal matters, including filing our reports to the Federal Election Commission, at cost. Shirley Richards, an accountant at one of the (then) Big Eight accounting firms in Portland, offered to do the accounting work *for free*. My personal secretary and good-right-hand, Dani Wade in Bend, became secretary to the campaign, handling all of our voluminous correspondence. Kris Rees stayed on as Finance Director. Bruce Amsbary, another Portland activist whose personal crusade was gay rights, became our office manager. And we hired Rob Johnson as our advance man. I had interviewed Rob back in Washington, D.C. and what had attracted me to him was his answer to one of my questions. He was as sick of the Reagan revolution as I was and, when I asked him why he was in this business, he assured me that he wouldn't rest "until the Democrats reclaim the White House!"

And we had also taken on two key consultants: Paul Maslin, then of Hickman-Maslin Associates of L.A., who did our polling; and the most important consultant of all, Joe Trippi of Washington, D.C., who was our "media consultant", that is, he created and produced our TV spots.

My thinking at the time was, "Who needs all these people? — and who needs all this *payroll*?" But, as she would turn out to be many times thereafter, Karen was right. Eventually, we added even more staff, some paid, some not.

Most of the key people weren't from Oregon. Almost all of them were young — to me, at 58, they were kids. Karen was only 27 — my daughter was older than that! Except for the consultants, almost all of them were under 30. Most of them worked for peanuts, for the cause. And, of course, most of us were strangers to one another. With Karen's firm but gentle hand, this group of young people turned into the finest political campaign staff in Oregon before it was over. And their chronological age belied their maturity, dedication, and intensity.

# # #

Our first event was our formal campaign kickoff, on March 5, 1990. We had planned a packed day. Our press release to all the newspapers and radio and TV stations outlined our hectic schedule. With the help of a friend with an airplane, we planned stops in four key towns: Bend, my hometown; Medford, a major timber town in southwestern Oregon; Eugene, the State's second largest city; and culminating in Portland, in time, we hoped, for the 6 o'clock news.

In Bend, we held our press event at Bend Research, the company I had co-founded. The only press coverage was the local newspaper, but everyone at the Company showed up to cheer me on.

Never an adept, spontaneous public speaker, I nevertheless wanted to wing my campaign-announcement speech: lots of passion; just be me. Overruled. Karen pointed out that this was a game of hardball. Any off-the-cuff misstatement, especially if taken out of context, could come back to haunt us later — could even be ruinous, if flagrant enough. So I wrote out my speech, accepted some changes ("just clarifications") from the brain trust, and read it. And, 100 minutes later and 150 miles away, I was reading it again, in front of a manufactured audience, at a labor union hall in Medford. And again in Eugene, and finally in Portland, in front of an impressive Lincoln statue in the "Park Blocks", in mid-town. By the fourth reading, I had it down pretty well, and could add some verve to it. It was at least up to Al Gore standards by then.

Press coverage? Well, we didn't make the evening news. And The Oregonian, the state's leading newspaper and the newspaper of record for Oregon, covered us, all right — on the page *after* the obituary page. Dan Walter, the press secretary, correctly concluded that getting any meaningful coverage of an unknown candidate by The Oregonian for a campaign against their beloved Mark Hatfield was going to take a lot of spade work on his part.

My first formal speech was a bust. It should have been a piece of cake, because it was given to a group of would-be friends. Each year, the leaders of the Oregon Democratic Party, including many elected officials, hold a weekend retreat. In 1990, it was held at Silver Falls State Park, not far from the state capitol in Salem. They were all there: former, present, and future mayors and members of the legislature; Party officials; powerbrokers. The guest of honor was James Carville, who wasn't as famous then as he was to become as Bill Clinton's principal political strategist for the '92 Presidential campaign, but a seasoned veteran with a wonderful wit, a great Cajun accent, and a great delivery.

I had been invited to speak. And I was scared. These people were pros. Political speech was their stock-in-trade, and most of them had given dozens of speeches and had heard hundreds. So, instead of winging it, as I probably should have, I wrote it out and then read it. The words weren't bad, but the delivery was awful: stumbles, missed lines, and worst of all, "dry mouth". What was I afraid of? These were my friends. What would happen when I was confronting strangers or, worse, a hostile group? I was to find out.

An early event took Rob Johnson, our advance man, and me to a senior center in Medford. I had only been to Medford a couple of times in my life, and just finding the meeting place was a challenge. When we finally got there, late, it was lunchtime. We needed the permission of the hostess to mingle with the folks. That done, Rob said, nonchalantly, "O.K., Harry, go work the room."

"Go what?"

"You know, work the room."

"But what does that mean?"

"It's easy. You just go from person to person, shake their hand, be sure you tell them your name and that you're running for the U.S. Senate. But be brief. Keep moving."

"But, Rob, they're eating lunch. Why would they want to meet me?"

"They don't want to meet *you*. You want to meet *them*. Now, go to it. And we have to leave here by no later than 1:30 to get to our next scheduled stop."

And so I did.

"Hello. Can I interrupt for a second? I'm Harry Lonsdale and I'm running for the U.S. Senate."

"What's your name again?"

"Lonsdale. Harry Lonsdale."

"Lonsberry? Why do you want to do a fool thing like that? Who are you running against?"

"Mark Hatfield."

"Hatfield? Why, he's a Republican and a good man, not like those other bums back in Washington. I've voted for him all my life."

Next.

"Hello. Can I interrupt for a second? My name is Harry Lonsdale, and I'm running for the United States Senate."

No response.

Next. Same opening spiel.

"You're not going to cut our Social Security, are you?"

"Nope."

Next.

"Are you a Republican or a Democrat?"

Next.

"Tell me, what's on your mind these days? What would you like to see changed back in Washington, D.C.?"

"First, throw those bums out. They're all a bunch of crooks. Then, fix our roads here. They're full of potholes. And then get these kids to shape up, stop smoking pot, and go to work."

"How do you feel about our forests?"

"Love 'em. I was a logger for 37 years. My father was a logger. My son was too, till those damned environmentalists closed down the mill. Now he can't find work, and his unemployment has about run out."

Next!

And so it went. I learned that most of those folks, like most folks everywhere, aren't concerned with the Founding Fathers or the American dream, or the ancient forests, or campaign finance reform, or the power of incumbency, or the military-industrial complex, or the rich getting richer, or our trade deficit with Japan, or even the national debt. They cared about local issues, the day-to-day. Former House Speaker "Tip" O'Neill once said that "all politics is local", and those friendly but skeptical people proved that to me, first hand.

I had "worked the room" much too slowly, stopping for extended chats with half of the people there. By 1:30, I wasn't even half way around the room. Still, at the urging of some of them, I danced with a few of the women after lunch, when the three-piece band struck up a '40s tune. We left late.

In the car, I said to Rob, "I don't think I picked up a single vote in there. Most of them were life-long Republicans. They loved Hatfield. Couldn't care less about what I was selling. This isn't working."

"Patience, Harry, patience. It will work. Just you wait and see. But you've got to move faster. Shake every hand. Don't worry about being polite. They'll talk forever, if you let them."

First lesson: Toughen up. This is business, not pleasure.

I faintly recalled watching our then-governor, Neil Goldschmidt, work a room. He was practiced. His secret, I realized, was to never actually stand still, but to keep his feet shuffling, ever so slowly, toward the next handshake. No conversations. No substance. Just keep moving, and smiling.

It's something I never really got the hang of.

# # #

Polling.

Now, I had heard about polling. "According to a recent Time/CNN poll, 76% of Americans attend church at least once a month," or "...58% of Americans admit to lying at least once in a while." But I'd never thought much about polls. Were they accurate? Who paid for them? Why? Like most people, I would read about a poll in the newspaper, tried to stick it in my mental file if there was a place to file it, and then turn the page.

But to an election campaign manager in a "modern campaign", to proceed without a poll would be like flying blindfolded. First comes the "base-line" poll, to establish some fundamental facts about the candidate, the opponent, the issues, and the mood of the people. Later on come updates and, finally, "tracking polls" in the final stages of a campaign, if you can afford them. Newspapers frequently do polls of their own. But from the point of view of the candidate, those come along much too late in the campaign—frequently when the race is already decided, and, besides, they don't ask the right questions for a candidate's purposes.

There are a handful of people in Oregon who do polling for a living, but none of them had the sort of statewide experience we were looking for. Enter Paul Maslin, then from L.A., who was an experienced and savvy pollster, who only polled for Democrats. My initial reaction, as in all of the newfangled electioneering stuff, was that we didn't need a poll. "I know who I am, and what I stand for, and why I'm running; and I know about Mark Hatfield; and I read the paper every day. Why do we have to spend $25,000 (of *my* money) on some fool poll?"

Well, we did. And there's no doubt that Maslin earned his money. The first thing he did was to come to Oregon, interview me, meet with the brain trust of our campaign—consisting of the management, plus an ad hoc kitchen cabinet of Portland-area political junkies—to learn about the issues and about what Oregonians were like. Then he went home and prepared the polling instrument. (The very word "instrument" told me that pollsters were convinced that they were doing science or something close to it.)

A typical base-line poll consists of several dozen questions. The first few are intended to weed out the non-voters and then to learn something about the respondent's background and status: gender, age, Democrat or Republican?, employed?, urban/rural, etc. Then come the meaty questions. "Which of these names do you recognize: Neil Goldschmidt, Harry Lonsdale, Mark Hatfield, Peter DeFazio (an Oregon Congressman), etc.?" Then, the first of several "horse race" questions: "There's a U.S. Senate race coming up here in Oregon this November. Mark Hatfield is the incumbent. Are you likely to vote for Hatfield or would you consider voting for someone else?" Then, some questions to introduce the not-so-hypothetical candidate. "If Mark Hatfield's opponent were a pro-choice, businessman, environmentalist, would you vote for Hatfield or the challenger?" Then some "push" questions: "If you knew that Hatfield was strongly pro-life and had voted in the Senate against all forms of abortion 16 times, would that make you more or less likely to vote for him?" Then, positive questions about Hatfield, to determine his perceived strengths. Similarly, positive and negative questions about the not-so-hypothetical candidate, me, to determine my perceived strengths and weaknesses. Finally, the "revote". "Knowing what you now know about Hatfield and about his hypothetical challenger, who would you vote for?"

Actually, I haven't done justice to the pollster's skills in this thumbnail sketch of the polling art. The questions are very carefully worded. The *order* of the questions is carefully considered. The results are carefully collated and broken down by demographic and other factors.

The polling is done over the telephone, usually by some telemarketing or public-opinion-survey organization, usually from out-of-state (so the callers have to be taught how to pronounce uniquely Oregon words, lest they tip themselves off as foreigners), usually over a two- or three-day period. All of the questions are scripted, and all the caller does is read the questions and note the answers.

The results that came back weren't unexpected. First, very few people knew my name. And those few that claimed they did, perhaps 3% of the respondents, were probably fibbing so as not to appear uninformed. A little work to do there, on name I.D. (A little work and a million dollars in TV advertising.) Second, Hatfield was popular, but he had some vulnerabilities, too. Incumbency was a decided disadvantage in the eyes of most voters, although still a huge advantage, operationally, to the incumbent running for re-election. And there were several specifics on which Hatfield scored poorly: being pro-life (or anti-choice) on the abortion issue was a positive for some voters but an important negative for an even larger group. For some, he was out-of-touch, and had been in Washington, D.C., too long and had lost his Oregon roots—he had become a Washington, D.C., insider. (Although I wasn't a native Oregonian, I had resided in the State a lot more than Hatfield had, in the previous 25 years.) Environmentalists didn't like him, and organized labor wasn't fond of him.

There was something to go on—not a lot, but something. Paul Maslin's conclusion was, "This is a winnable race. You've got some work to do to become known by the voters, but your issues are good ones and if you can get your message to the voters, you can win. But it won't be easy."

I was skeptical. When was the last time that a pollster, who has just been presented with a handsome check for his work and who hopes to receive more of the same, has said, "This is not a winnable race. Give up. Go home"? Partly because we wanted to believe his advice, and partly because the polling questions and the answers thereto seemed reasonable, we were encouraged.

We came up with three basic issues that we would use throughout the campaign: protection of the environment, especially the ancient forests of the Northwest; choice, on the abortion question, which clearly differentiated myself from Mark Hatfield; and campaign finance reform, including the need to break the stranglehold of Political Action

Committees (PACs) and special-interest money on federal elections and on our federal officials post-election. Our positions on these issues were, respectively, stop logging the ancient forests, stop clear-cutting, and stop exporting our unprocessed logs to Japan and elsewhere; the right of choice is fundamental to women, guaranteed by the Supreme Court in the *Roe vs. Wade* decision, (and something I believed in fervently); and PAC contributions should be outlawed, and free TV time should be granted to qualified candidates for federal office, as was the case in almost every other industrialized country.

# # #

In the winter of 1990, our only concern was winning the primary election in May, and, along the way, building up my name identification with Oregon voters. The first question Karen Olick wanted answered was, "Who else is in this race and *do they have any money?*" By the filing deadline, there were six of us in the Democratic primary and two—Hatfield and a "tree-hugger" Republican named Randy Prince—in the Republican primary.

We were six white males, five of us virtually unknown, challenging a popular four-term incumbent Senator. Steve Anderson had run unsuccessfully for almost every major elected office in Oregon: Governor, Secretary of State, the House of Representatives, and the U.S. Senate (against Hatfield). Like the rest of us, Steve had never held elected office before, but based on his previous candidacies, he was the leading contender because he had at least some name familiarity with the voters. The four other unknowns were Frank Clough, Neale Hyatt, Bob Reuschlein, and Brooks Washburne.

Anderson was 75 years old, and a practicing attorney. He has since passed away. Clough was a retired pilot and commercial beekeeper. Hyatt, 48, quit his job at Bi-Mart, a discount store, to devote full time to running for office. Reuschlein, 40, was an economic researcher by profession, whose main campaign issue was the military-industrial complex. Washburne was a 75-year-old retired truck driver. Washburne and Clough were the mystery men of the campaign. I don't believe that I ever met them, nor do I remember them ever being mentioned in the newspapers between the time they filed and election day.

The other four of us appeared at candidate forums put on by some of the Democratic committees around the state and by the League of Women Voters. These forums, although very lightly attended, were two-way streets. The local Democrats wanted to look us over, and we wanted to stimulate them to get involved in the race, to convince them as early as possible that Hatfield could be defeated, and Oregon could finally claim at least one Democratic Senator after more than two decades of Republicans Hatfield and Packwood.

The people who attend these Democratic forums aren't your typical voters. They are the true believers, the "Yellow Dog" Democrats, mostly seniors, labor union members, the far left. What *they* wanted to know was how liberal were *we*? Were we true FDR New Dealers or had we back-slid to the political center? Their questions and comments could be tough, occasionally brutal, frequently personal, sometimes loaded: a little "toughening up" exercise for the candidates. But not much fun for me. I came to respect the three other serious candidates. Our positions on the key issues facing Oregon were surprisingly similar; pro-choice, pro-environment, socially liberal, fiscally conservative. Anderson and Hyatt were good public speakers, probably better than I was, at least in the beginning. Our face-to-face meetings were usually cordial-to-friendly, and the only shots they took at me in our public debates were that I was rich and was trying to buy the election, charges I was to hear many times in the ensuing months.

# # #

During the primary campaign, while I thought I was busy, I was only coasting compared with the stretch run of the general election campaign to come.

While no two days of campaigning were ever the same, some order was established early on. Breakfast: a sweet roll and a glass of milk or a hot chocolate with the troops at the campaign headquarters. Or, if one could be found, a meeting with a potential contributor, or maybe a key volunteer. Dan Walter had the press "clips" photocopied early in the day, more, actually, than I could hope to assimilate: the leading Oregon newspapers, The New York Times, and if there was anything relevant on the tube the evening before, a scan of the video "clips". Then followed a brief strategy session, a preview of the day's schedule with Carrie Goux, the scheduler, and we were on the road.

Where? Anywhere and everywhere: to meet with environmental groups, or women's groups, to either deliver the "stump speech" or to seek their endorsement; to senior centers to work the room; to a hideaway office to make fund-raising calls for 3 hours (almost every day, Sundays included); to Rotary lunches for the stump speech; to my apartment for some time alone to prepare a position paper on some key subject; to just walk the streets and shake hands, to cafes to shake more hands; to Saturday markets to shake *more* hands; to press conferences; to meet with leaders of the Greek community or the Black community or the gay and lesbian community; to return phone calls, to, well, you get the idea. Lunch? On the fly, somewhere.

Dinner? The best option would be a meal with a potential major contributor. More likely, it was cold pizza and warm Pepsi with the crew back at the campaign office. Then followed answering the mail, which was voluminous even in the early days.

Finally, by 10 or 11 P.M., I was off to bed, only to start it all over again at 7:30 the next morning, six or seven days a week.

Some people seem to thrive on large groups of people. Bill Clinton, for example, seems to love being with people every waking hour, the more the merrier. Not me. I have always cherished my alone time. And in a statewide election campaign, there simply *is* none, unless the candidate insists on it. After a few weeks on the campaign trail, I remember going to my one-room apartment at the end of the day, taking off my clothes, turning out the light, crawling into bed, pulling the covers up over my head, cocoon-like, and saying to myself, out loud, "They can't get me in here!" In time, I came to lay down the law with Karen Olick: I insisted on one weekend a month, at my home in Bend, in my own little bed. It kept me alive.

# # #

Press Secretary Dan Walter's job was two-fold. First, he had to help me and the rest of the campaign staff in getting our message out, that is, in telling Oregonians where we stood on the issues, and how we differed from Hatfield in some key areas. It meant he had to become familiar with members of the media all around the state, overcome their natural cynicism toward politicians, and get them to print, or show on the evening news, an accurate view of our stuff — filtered, as it always is, by the media reporters themselves.

But a second job, equally important, was simply to get my name out there, to get me known. "They don't vote for you if they don't know who you are", and there are only three ways to become known — actually, it's probably only two. You could, in principle, meet every voter and become known that way. But even in a relatively small state, population-wise, like Oregon, it takes 500,000-600,000 votes or more to win a statewide election. There simply aren't enough hours in the day to meet that many people, even if you could round them all up into one huge bunch. So there are only two really effective ways to become known to the voters: free media, sometimes called "earned media"; and paid media, i.e. TV, radio, or newspaper ads. Lawn signs and bumper-stickers? Forget 'em. Everyone uses them and they're fun, but they simply don't convince anyone to vote for you. Billboards, too, have been shown to be well down the list in terms of bang for the buck. We didn't do any billboard ads. Finally, there's the mail. It's less effective than TV in general in a statewide election, but it's essential for reaching and convincing some people.

We sent out a ton of letters, hundreds of thousands of them. On mailing days, a dozen or more volunteers would be called in to stuff envelopes. I stuffed more than a few myself. One thing that's essential for a mailing is a mailing list. It was a problem that would have stumped me. But not the pros. "Lists? You just buy 'em." And it was true. There are mailing lists for almost any type of American you can think of, and almost all of them are for sale, at a surprisingly low cost. (That knowledge about lists certainly changed my attitude toward filling out *any* business form with my name and address.)

But Dan Walter's job was to get us in the news for free. It wasn't easy. Dan and the brain trust would sit up half the night trying to find the "hook," the magic ingredient that would produce some news coverage when we sent out a press release or when we called a press conference. The "hook" gives editors a reason to run the story that day, a reason to send the reporter to talk to you rather than to someone else. Every major newspaper in the U.S. gets dozens or even hundreds of press releases every day, from a wide variety of sources, and almost all of them wind up straight in the round file. There are also press conferences, of course.

But how do you get the press, including the electronic media, to even show up? The competition for news coverage is fierce: wars, fires, murders, rapes, bank heists, etc. all get top billing. We worked, and worked hard, but with discouraging results, at least during the primary campaign.

There's an art to bringing off a successful press conference, assuming the press even shows up. My biggest problem was being too talkative. The word in the game of politics is to "stay on message." I was coached to stick to our three major issues, and not get sucked in by the reporters' off-message questions. Olick's advice: "Don't answer *their* questions; make *your* statement. No matter what they say or ask, make your statement!"

Well, I couldn't. Maybe it was my science background. But all my life, when asked a straightforward question, I tried to supply a straightforward answer. It's inherent in human nature. But not for politicians, who have learned to do anything *but* give a straightforward answer, particularly if it was going to cost them some votes.

One of my lifetime frustrations with politicians, in fact, has been that they *don't* answer direct questions. I think Americans are begging for real answers to the tough questions of the day.

My hero among TV reporters has been Sam Donaldson. When Sam, indignant, says for the third time, "But, Senator, you haven't answered my question. Let me repeat it for you..." I want to jump out of my chair and kiss the TV. Even if the Senator *never does* answer the question, at least Sam has exposed him as an evader. Keep it up, Sam!

The bottom line for me in those press conferences was that, with rare exceptions, I was too candid. Our message got buried.

# # #

What is all the free press worth? A great deal. Let's first ask, "how much does it cost to have every voter know your name and some basic facts about you?" The answer is about a dollar per voter. When Ross Perot ran for President in 1992, it was reported that he spent about $65 million of his own money, almost all of it on TV infomercials and TV spots. When the campaign was over, 100 million American voters knew his name, what he looked and sounded like, and where he stood on several key issues. So he spent something less than a dollar per voter to achieve that familiarity. He received 19 million votes, so he spent about $3 per vote. But he also benefited from a great deal of free media *once he had bought the paid media.* The free press doesn't really kick in until a goodly number of people know you. There's only so much space in a newspaper, or so much time on a 30-minute TV news show. And the media aren't going to waste any of that precious, expensive space on nobodies. Put it all together, and it's about one dollar per voter to become known. Some successful candidates spend less, and some unsuccessful candidates spend a lot more. (Here are some extremes: Al Checchi, California gubernatorial candidate in 1998, spent something like $60 per vote, and lost! Ralph Nader, in his 1996 very low budget presidential campaign, spent less than a *penny* per vote. He lost, too. Nader obviously benefited from many years of free press that gave him considerable name I.D.)

And so, any time Dan Walter got the TV news cameras to show up we were saving a whale of a lot of money, even if the reporters' questions were off-message, and even if I screwed up.

Of course, all the free press and all the paid press in the world won't guarantee 100% name familiarity. I once had the pleasure of spending an hour with former President Jimmy Carter. He was fly-fishing on the Williamson River, near the tiny town of Ft. Klamath in southern Oregon, and a mutual friend had set up the meeting. President Carter travels with a Secret Service escort, as all former Presidents do. The previous day, President Carter had walked through the only store in Ft. Klamath, the Mercantile. The place probably didn't draw twenty customers a week, but that day eight guys in suits walked through with Carter. The proprietor, an octogenarian, asked the last Secret Service agent as he was going out the door, who all those people were.

The agent responded, "Didn't you recognize him? That was Jimmy Carter."

Proprietor, "Really, who's he?"

Agent, "The former President of the United States!"

Proprietor, "Really? Where's he from?"

There are no guarantees.

# # #

During the primary phase, the person "in the street" may be unaware that there's an election coming up, but the special interest groups make it their business to find out who's running and to decide who they're backing. Often, they pick their candidates by means of questionnaires and, sometimes, by in-person interviews. It was amazing to me just how many such special interest groups there are. There are the Realtors, the home-builders, the League of Women Voters, organized labor, AIPAC (a pro-Israel group), animal-rights groups, gay and lesbian groups, education groups, environmental groups, pro-life and pro-choice groups, and, of course, the National Rifle Association (NRA), and many more. Reading the questionnaires from these organizations, it is ultra-clear exactly what answers they want, and there's the temptation, of course, to fudge and score a perfect 100% on the questionnaires from organizations you favor.

Some of the questionnaires were simply outrageous. The one from the NRA was shocking, in terms of the rights they believe are granted to Americans under the Second Amendment. I glanced at it, decided that I would score a big, fat zero if I bothered to fill it out, and chucked it in the wastebasket. Early in the primary campaign, I remembered a heckler in an audience asking me where I stood on the Second Amendment. The truth was, I didn't even know what the Second Amendment *was*. I soon learned, at least this guy's version. That was my first warning to go back and read the entire Constitution, including all (the then) 26 amendments, which I hadn't done since high school, if ever.

I didn't get the NRA endorsement.

Newspaper endorsements aren't like organization endorsements. The major newspapers invite the candidate to a meeting of its editorial board, consisting of all those who write their editorials, plus the editor-in-chief and the publisher. The questions are wide-ranging, in-depth, and generally fair, although they do carry with them the newspaper's biases. Up to that time, for example, The Oregonian had endorsed every Republican candidate for president since Abraham Lincoln, except for Barry Goldwater in 1964.

I was endorsed for the Democratic nomination, even before the primary, by several newspapers in the state, including The Oregonian, not necessarily because they thought I was the best candidate but just because they thought I was going to win the primary, because I had some of my own money to spend. And NARAL, the National Abortion Rights Action League, as it was then known, did an early endorsement of me.

Endorsements wouldn't be so easy to come by in the general election.

# # #

One thing the candidate doesn't lack is advisors, and I had more than my share. Many of them were intelligent, well informed, and politically savvy. I'm eternally indebted to those good people who helped. But the ones you tend to remember best are the kooks and the pests: people who had never held office, who had never even *run* for office, had never even been involved in any election campaign. But they sure were free with their advice and they sure knew how I could win! One guy, with no political experience, wanted us to pay him $2000 a month for his advice, and he'd contribute half of his first month's paycheck back to the campaign! Another guy "sure wanted to help" but only if I changed the license plates on my car! It seems that the numbers on my plate had some religious connotation, and he "sure couldn't work for anyone with *those* license plates". And there were those people who wanted me to agree with them on *every* issue. "Harry, you're a great guy, and I love just about everything you stand for. I really want to work on your campaign, and so do my friends. I know that we can deliver Josephine County for you this fall. But there's just one thing. You have to reverse your position on _____." (fill in the blank: abortion, gun control, forest protection, whatever).

# # #

Early in the campaign, I had an enlightening conversation with Brock Evans. Evans was then vice president of National Audubon, and in the late '80s he had run for a seat in the U.S. House of Representatives from Seattle. He lost in a close election, but he had been through everything I was going through. He offered this observation: "Harry, you're going through a real educational experience. You're going to learn a lot about people. Some people that you *know* you can count on, some of your best friends, will desert you. But others, total strangers, will come out of the woodwork and work their butts off for you." He was right on both counts.

# # #

The pundits and the press, who were certainly more savvy early on than I, knew it was all over in the Democratic primary when we started running media consultant Joe Trippi's well done TV spots statewide.

When you see a candidate's commercials on TV, with the catchy music, the American flag shown subtly in the background, and the relaxed forthrightness of the candidate, you think that's the real world, that's just the candidate doing her/his thing on a typical day in her/his life. But it's anything *but* the real world. First, the location where the spot is to be produced is carefully chosen. A studio is best, because it's a controlled environment. If it's done outdoors, as ours were, hours are spent looking for the ideal spot: idyllic, quiet, scenic, preferably with some special feature, but not *so* special that it detracts from the candidate. Then there's the script. In a thirty-second spot, even if the candidate or a paid professional voice is speaking the whole time, there's only enough time for maybe 50-75 words, so each word is carefully chosen, argued over, and finally agreed upon. Then there's the haircut, the clean shave, make-up to remove those facial lines and any trace of perspiration, and the right clothes. Then there's how you *say* the words, the emphasis, your facial expression, your hand movements, if any, your posture, the pauses, the opening, the closing. It's not unusual for 10-20 "takes" to be made before the producer/director is satisfied. I remember one particularly arduous spot that Trippi, the sound man, the camera man, and I were suffering through. After 15 takes and nothing worth keeping, we were all pretty exasperated. Trippi saved the day when he told me that a prior client of his, who became governor of West Virginia, Gaston Caperton III, required 187 takes before he got two spots down pat. So, relatively speaking, I was doing just fine.

Sometimes a voice other than the candidate's is used. There are men and women scattered around the country who make a good living reading those scripted messages for political candidates, beer-and-soap-and-car ads, and all the rest. I had no idea whose the voice was on my spots.

Then there's the music. Again, it's an entire industry in itself. Any mid-size-town radio station that makes its own commercials has an enormous repertoire of various sounds: music of all sorts, from triumphal to terrifying, but more, too: bird calls, car doors slamming, waterfalls, airplanes, the works.

Finally, there's the editing, a time-consuming and laborious job: what to use, what to toss. Even small-town TV studios allow the operator to start and stop a given sequence on the exact frame he or she wants (at 30 frames per second). And, of course, they can dub in scenes from file video, stock material, or special effects (animation, turning the image sideways, "morphing" one face into another) or a thousand different tricks, *all* to get and hold the viewer's attention and to have them remember at least something from the spot. It's an entire industry.

Our spots were well done, effective, and expensive to run. We spent a total of about $300,000 on the primary, most of it my own money, and most of it was spent on TV ads. Our Democratic opponents spent virtually nothing.

Two weeks before the primary, The Oregonian, the Eugene Register-Guard, and the Salem Statesman-Journal all predicted that Mark Hatfield and I would be the winners of the Republican and Democratic primaries. The Democratic Party back in Washington, D.C., as represented by the Democratic Senatorial Campaign Committee, also predicted me the winner and to back up their bet they paid for $17,000 worth of our TV ads — after we had bought about $200,000 worth on our own. That infuriated the other Democratic candidates, as well it should have.

And the newspapers were right. On Election Day, May 15, it was strictly no contest. On the Democratic side, we pulled 64% of the vote, Anderson 13%, Clough 3%, Hyatt 8%, Reuschlein 6%, and Washburne 5%. On the Republican side, it was Hatfield with 79% and Prince with 21%. We figured that virtually all of the Prince votes were really anti-Hatfield votes among the Republicans, since Prince spent no money and was therefore virtually unknown. The voter turnout was quite respectable, about 46% — but it usually is for primaries in Oregon.

It was a big victory for us. Even though Democratic registrants in Oregon outnumber Republicans, and Independents can't vote in the primary, more Republicans than Democrats voted in the 1990 Senate primary, which was a cause for some worry. There are 36 counties in Oregon, and we won in 35 of them. The only county we lost was a small county in the northeastern part of the State where they don't get any of the Oregon television stations, and so we hadn't advertised there. Most of the voters there facing their ballots had never heard of *any* of us, and the result was a near 6-way split. First lesson: It's TV ads, stupid!

And I immediately began to wonder: will Hatfield do to me in the general election what I did to the other Democrats in the primary: bury me with money?

# # #

After the primary, there was an inevitable let down. We had won, but it was still a long time to the general election on Nov. 6. We actually took a couple of days off. Dan Walter and I even went fishing for a couple of hours.

The euphoria and the down-time were brief. It was summertime, a time for county fairs, parades, *people to meet, hands to shake, money to raise, speeches to give*.

Most cities and towns have a reputation for being either conservative or liberal: San Diego, staunchly conservative; New York City and Boston, flaming liberal. It's true in Oregon, as well. The conservatives in Oregon tend to be from the eastern part of the state, where ranching, logging, mining, and wheat farming are the major income-producers. And the farther east you go in Oregon, the more conservative it becomes. Wallowa County, one of the most beautiful places in America and one of the most remote, holds the record, from my observations, for the most conservative, resistant-to-change part of Oregon.

Portland is generally considered the most liberal town in Oregon, although university-town Eugene would also lay claim to that title. But they're both fighting over second place. The most liberal town in Oregon, bar none, is Ashland, home of Southern Oregon University and the renowned Oregon Shakespeare Festival.

Ashland has an annual 4th of July parade, and in 1990 I walked in it. Some supporters held a large "LONSDALE FOR SENATE" banner as I walked, so that people would know who I was. Frequently, candidates, especially well-known incumbents, ride in a car and simply wave to the crowd. Not this candidate; I worked both sides of the street.

I will remember that day as long as I live. It was euphoric. Not only did they know me, they seemed to love me. Hands, from the third row back in the crowd, reaching out for a shake. Pats on the back. Kind words, encouraging words. And the *piece de resistance* was a large group of young people, students, I suppose, hanging out of second-story windows or literally sitting on roof tops, shouting my name, chanting HAR-ry, HAR-ry, HAR-ry. I could understand, at that moment, how politicians can get hooked on this stuff.

Too bad I wasn't running for the Senator from *Ashland*!

# # #

I was never very good at public speaking. To try to improve myself, I once started to attend a Toastmasters group, but I dropped out after only a couple of meetings when I saw how they attempted to overcome stage fright: by making you stand up and do the most embarrassing and, to me, stupid things. I should have toughed it out, for I had plenty of public speaking to do.

I got help from two sources. First, Karen Olick's "significant other" and husband-to-be, a brilliant young man named John Gibson, quit his successful job at a topflight law firm in Washington, D.C., to join our campaign as speechwriter and issues-researcher. John had done some campaign work before and he became a key contributor to the brain trust. Good friend Joyce Tsongas offered to be my speech coach, for free. Joyce headed her own trial-consulting firm in Portland and she had excellent credentials in public speaking. I learned that there are many seemingly incidental facets to a successful speech. "Don't move your feet. Pretend your shoes are screwed down to the floor. Don't bring your hand up to scratch those facial itches, or to run your hand through your hair. The two most important sentences you will say in any speech are the first and the last; make them bold. And practice, Practice, PRACTICE, so that it will appear that you're winging it even when you're reading it. Best of all, memorize the whole speech and don't read it at all!" I never could. And I never really got over my "dry mouth" problem. But I did get better with their help. When it really counted, I was now up to the job.

The first important test was the annual Oregon AFL-CIO convention, held that summer. It's common knowledge that labor unions customarily endorse Democrats, and I naively thought that their endorsement of me was a given. But politics makes strange bedfellows. Some of the major member unions in the AFL-CIO were the Carpenters and Joiners Union, the Pulp and Paper Workers, and the Woodworkers. Because I wanted to sharply reduce the timber cut levels, and because Hatfield had been instrumental in keeping the cut level high over the years, those folks were not my allies, and they were very influential in the labor movement because of their large membership.

I made my pitch to them, in front of a group of a thousand or more, on conventional New Deal issues, but they weren't buying. Speaking style didn't count for much. What they wanted to know was what I was going to do for *them*, specifically, as a U.S. Senator. My greatest strength, I felt, was that I was strongly in favor of no permanent replacement of striking workers. As things stood then — and still stand today — employers could legally hire permanent replacements for their striking workers to keep their plants open. It gave all the power in labor negotiations to management. I felt that it was grossly unfair. But that didn't earn me their endorsement. Besides, they knew Hatfield. His labor voting record was only so-so, but he was an insider with a lot of clout. Many labor union PACs had contributed to his campaigns in the past.

Even though I didn't realize it at the time, I came into that convention with some heavy baggage. It came from a letter I once wrote to then-Congressman Ron Wyden. On one of his trips back to Oregon in the mid-'80s, Wyden had called together a group of small-business people, including me, to discuss our country's international competitiveness, or lack of same. He served at that time on the House Small Business Committee. We all offered Wyden ideas at the meeting, but he asked us to follow up with a letter, summarizing our off-hand remarks. My letter addressed the issue of U.S. productivity *vs.* that of the rest of the world. At that time, the average pay for U.S. manufacturing workers was the highest in the world, even though their productivity wasn't, for a variety of reasons. (Things have changed dramatically since then. In 2001, the U.S. ranks No. 1 in the world in worker productivity, mainly because we're now outworking the rest of the world. According to the International Labor Organization of the U.N., Americans now work a month a year more than Japanese workers; *three* months a year more than German workers.) My letter to Wyden included the language "...the American worker is overpaid..." relative to workers in other countries, on a productivity basis. It wasn't the best choice of wording. Once copies of that letter got in the hands of organized labor in Oregon, as it inevitably had to, I was even less popular with big labor than Republican Hatfield. It took a 2/3 vote for them to endorse, and it took a massive floor effort by the few labor friends we had to deny Hatfield the endorsement. In the end, they did a "no endorsement". It was a blow. It was our first lesson that most organizations will endorse incumbents, in whom they have invested time or money or both in establishing a relationship, unless there is a very compelling reason to go with the challenger. Incumbents already have power, and their incumbency alone makes it likely they'll win. Party affiliation ain't what it used to be.

Our next stop was the annual convention of the Oregon Education Association, the teachers union, and the largest labor organization and the largest lobbying group in the state. Here, again, I thought I had a persuasive case to make. I was about as pro-education as you could get. In my speech to their convention, I spoke about my two uneducated parents who pushed me hard all through school and college, and about two outstanding high school teachers who had a lot to do with my career, and about what a solid education had done for me. Besides, I was a Democrat and 70% of the teachers in Oregon are Democrats.

But being pro-education isn't the same as being pro-teachers union. I was generally empathetic to the plight of the teachers: classes were far too big; salaries were low, considering what we expected of them; and their jobs had come to encompass a lot more than just teaching the subject matter—we asked them to be disciplinarians (without authority) and even baby-sitters in the lower grades. I thought I gave them my best speech to date, but it really didn't matter. If they needed a reason to vote against me, I gave it to them when I spoke in favor of merit pay, the notion that there should be a monetary reward for good performance in the teaching profession, just as there is in every other job. Oregon teachers seem to hate the idea.

Karen and the crew had worked that convention hard: banners, balloons, handouts, even a candidate's reception the evening before. She even went so far as to have the luncheon fortune cookies made up with the same message inside each one (including Hatfield's): "Lonsdale will win in November." I didn't know it at the time, but the endorsement votes had actually been cast in the individual school districts around the state weeks before. My speech was well received, but whatever I did that day didn't matter. In the end, it was Hatfield in a breeze: he took 80+% of the vote, and the endorsement.

When it was all over, and we had lost, I saw Karen crumpled in an overstuffed chair, exhausted and looking defeated for the first (and only) time.

# # #

There were some highs to go with the lows. One of Oregon's outstanding Democrats, Gerry Cogan, agreed to co-chair our campaign. It was an honorary job, but Gerry was strongly supportive and he had a lot of friends. And the late Maurine Neuberger, Oregon's first and only woman U.S. Senator, agreed to co-chair. Maurine was already frail and in her 80s, but her principles and her spirit remained as strong as ever.

Nationally, the League of Conservation Voters endorsed us. LCV is politically the most active of the environmental groups, and Jim Maddy, then the executive director in Washington, D.C., came out to Portland and held a press conference to announce their endorsement. And Kate Michelman, head of NARAL, came to Oregon twice to renew the endorsement they had made in the primary, and to be the draw at fund raisers.

# # #

Most of us have heroes of one type or another. Our parents, sports figures, war heroes, even political figures, whom we refer to as statesmen (and women). I've been a hero worshipper all my life. When I was growing up, it was Jackie Robinson, whom I admired for standing up to all the abuse from the bigoted fans and players when professional baseball was integrated.

Heroes come in all stripes. There was one I won't ever forget. The occasion was the annual Oregon Boys State convention. Each year, an outstanding male student is selected from each high school student body to attend Boys State. Usually, it's someone with political interests. All 50 states have Boys State conventions, I believe, and some have Girls State conventions as well. (The famous photograph of Bill Clinton shaking John Kennedy's hand was taken when Clinton represented the Arkansas Boys State group at the White House.)

I was asked to attend the Boys State convention in 1990 and to debate the most important question in Oregon: the future of our forests. My debate opponent was Jim Geisinger, a long-time paid employee and lobbyist for the timber industry. The debate was held in a large lecture hall on the University of Oregon campus in Eugene, in front of about 300 of Oregon's best and brightest. We each made 15-minute opening statements. Geisinger was good. He had been debating this subject formally and informally for years. He knew how many jobs the timber industry accounted for, directly and indirectly, the payrolls involved and how those payrolls kept many a small town in Oregon alive, and how many Americans lived in houses made out of wood. I had some pretty persuasive arguments, too, including the fact that current timber production levels were totally unsustainable and that many of the jobs were seasonal. But my coup de grace, I thought, was a powerful three-by-five-foot aerial photograph of an enormous clearcut in Oregon.

After the 15-minute opening arguments, the debate was opened up to questions from the floor. The first question was for me. It came from a young man who was obviously from a timber family living in a timber town. The question was sharp-edged. I responded. The next question was also for me, even sharper this time, from another timber-family member. I responded. A dozen hands shot up, and the next 12 questions in a row, increasingly belligerent, were all for me! I began to look for the door.

Finally, when it appeared that their heat had dissipated, one young man, sitting near the back of the room, raised his hand, was recognized, stood up, and with an obviously quavering voice, defended my position and asked a good question of Geisinger. Then came another for Geisinger, and another, and another—about 12 in a row! What wasn't apparent initially was that the room was about equally divided between environmentalists and pro-timber students. And we would never have known that had not that young man spoken up.

I learned a lot from him. I wish I had gotten his name. He's one of my heroes. To go against the flow, to speak out for a certain point of view when you believe the entire group opposes you, and they're hostile to boot, takes great courage. How many of us have it?

# # #

Campaigning wasn't all work. At the end of almost every day I had the opportunity of meeting with our young staff, finding out who they were, and why they were in this battle. They were almost all in their 20s, but surprisingly savvy politically. They cared a great deal about their country, and felt that under Reagan and Bush (the elder) we were headed in the wrong direction. They worked all hours of the day and night, for little pay. Most of them came from very middle-class families. When I visited the DSCC back in Washington, D.C., I found the same esprit de corps, and the same idealistic, youthful optimism.

Late in the summer, my spirits flagged badly. Fund raising wasn't going well at all, we weren't getting any press, and I had the feeling we couldn't win. A poll had appeared in The Oregonian in late August that really knocked me down: Hatfield 63%, Lonsdale 27%. We weren't going to just lose, it was going to be a blowout. I began to just go through the motions, and the staff noticed it. One morning I went to the campaign office for my usual breakfast sweet roll and carton of milk and found the door to the office locked. It was dark inside. That had never happened before. Someone was always there ahead of me each morning. With no schedule available for the day, I went back to my apartment, and returned later that morning, to the same locked door. Finally, I called Karen's apartment.

She was there. They were *all* there, having a hamburger barbecue. Their attitude was, if I wasn't working, neither were they! They had gone on *strike*. I had a heart-to-heart with them, was pumped up by them, and went back to work full-force. I realized that this wasn't just a job for them. It was a crusade.

# # #

One day, Dan Walter and I were driving back to Portland from an event in Ontario, in eastern Oregon. I was pooped, as usual. Dan was driving. As I awoke from one of my frequent cat-naps, we were approaching the small town of John Day. I spotted a small hand-painted sign by the side of the road, "Fresh Home Made Pies".

"Dan, stop the car!"

We had our choice, and we chose boysenberry. We drove into the center of John Day, a town of about 2000 people, looking for some green grass and a place to devour this prize. We found the park, with a swimming pool full of frolicking kids. "Oh, to be that carefree again", I thought.

"Dan, I don't have any utensils, but I do have my tiny pocket knife to cut it up with. Mind if we just use our hands?"

In less than 15 minutes, that pie was gone, eaten straight from the paper pie plate we had bought it on.

Slowly, we climbed back in the car, barreling toward Portland, daydreaming about that warm boysenberry pie.

# # #

To broaden my perspectives on Oregon's No. 1 problem—the timber issue, or as the environmentalists would say, the *forest* issue—I visited several wood-products plants: the James River paper mill in Wauna, the Pope & Talbot paper mill in Harrisburg, a veneer plant in Springfield, and others. Mostly, it was handshaking at the plant gate during shift changes, followed by a tour and maybe a stump speech during the lunch break, focusing on their issue. I didn't learn much except that these were hardworking people, worried about their future, and that many of them lived close to the edge. Wood products, like most extractive industries, is a seasonal, up-and-down business.

But my visit to the Roseburg Forest Products mill in Riddle was special. Riddle is a town of only about 1200 people, and you wouldn't call it prosperous. It's famous for having the only operating nickel-extraction plant in the U.S. But the largest employer in town by far was the lumber mill.

I was invited to speak to their local woodworkers union, at the close of work one day. It was a group of perhaps 20-25 people, men and women, tired from a hard day's work. They knew going in that I was an environmentalist, and enviros. weren't particularly welcome in Oregon's small mill towns, then or now. Still, I gave them my by-now standard pitch: we're overcutting, can't keep it up indefinitely, we're sending our raw logs to Japan (for the higher price) instead of processing them here, we needed to diversify our industrial base in Oregon, create new jobs, ...

I wasn't sure what kind of reception I would receive. I was talking long-range, theoretical stuff; they were thinking short-range, lunch-bucket, job-security stuff. Still, it was one of the best exchanges I experienced during the campaign. To start with, they were *polite*, which wasn't always the case in my statewide travels. And further, they were environmentalists, too, and proud of it. They told me of their love of fishing, hunting, hiking, and camping in the woods. Before long, we had all let our hair down and were doing some bonding. They knew we were overcutting the forests; they knew it better than I did, because they lived in the middle of what was once a great forest. And they hated clear-cuts, too.

Their attitudes ran like this: "Job diversification? Give us a break! We've worked in this mill, most of us, for 10-20 years. They've been downsizing for three years now. Every week, another one, two, or five people aren't here anymore. And there *is* no other work within 25 miles of here, and what work there is is being downsized, too. What are we supposed to do? If this plant closes, we've had it. Our homes aren't fancy, but we own 'em, along with the bank. And without this plant, our homes aren't worth a plug nickel. And what about the school,..."

How could you not be moved? Answers, Harry, these people want answers! The sad truth was that the most likely answer was that many of them would have to move away, unless the plant owners, those who had made a lot of profit over the years from their employees' labor, rescued them with new jobs. But the plant owners, in most Oregon mill towns, live far away and don't really give a rip about those people who work in their mills. Labor is just a commodity to many of them.

Without my being able to bring closure to the discussion, the meeting ended. The union leader, a strong but friendly woman who ran the meeting, took me aside afterwards and, concerned about the image the outside world had of the wood-products industry, said "Mr. Lonsdale, as you travel around the state, please tell everyone that we're not bad people. We're good people." And they are.

As I was leaving the plant site, a man in his late 30s put his hand on my arm and told me about his teenage daughter, smart as a whip, first in her class in high school, and real college material. "If this plant closes, she'll never make it to college. Then what's her future?"

# # #

The summer was winding down. I continued my almost totally unsuccessful fund-raising efforts by visiting known major Democratic contributors from around the U.S. A "major contributor" is one who could, if so inclined, contribute $1000, the legal limit proscribed by the Federal Election Commission. Before the race was over I had made fund-raising trips to Los Angeles (3), San Francisco (2), Seattle (2), New York City (2), and Washington, D.C. (2). They were almost a complete bust. We probably didn't take in the cost of the trips. Those people were hip. They had seen the poll numbers, and they weren't plunking down their good money on some long shot.

But not all the news was bad. The late David Brower, one of my heroes and the senior statesman among environmentalists around the world, came to Portland to do a major fund-raising event for me. So did Denis Hayes, another champion of the environmental movement and the national organizer of the first Earth Day in 1970. And so did ex-vice presidential candidate Geraldine Ferraro. She knew, even better than I, that candidates far behind in August can still pull out a victory in November, *if they have the money*. And Kate Michelman returned to Oregon on my behalf.

Worried about the poll numbers, we carried out some "focus groups", then a relatively new part of the candidate's arsenal. In a focus group, there is a moderator and a small group of perhaps 8-10-12 people carefully chosen to be typical people: the right age and gender distribution, no hard radicals from either side of the spectrum. Voters. People familiar with the issues. A blend of working people, business people, retirees. The purpose is to look for both candidates' strengths and weaknesses, and to define people's hot button issues. We held two focus groups in Medford, southern Oregon timber country, and two in Portland. Paul Maslin, our pollster, was the moderator for each.

I was able to watch the whole thing. It's done with the aid of a one-way glass, behind which we sat. The participants are told in advance that we were there but, after an initial warm-up period wherein the moderator gained their trust, they seemed to forget all about us. Focus groups, like polls, have now become sophisticated vehicles for studying public opinion on a wide variety of topics.

I learned a lot. The media, and particularly the print-press, may have lionized Mark Hatfield over the years, making him into Oregon's "Prince". But the public sure wasn't buying it! "Just one more politician." "Aloof." "Too goddam religious for me." "Sure, he's done some good stuff for Oregon. He *should* have, he's been back there long enough." "I bet *he's* made plenty!" (I don't think so, actually). "And what about that Tsakos affair? He was let off too easy on that."

The "Tsakos affair" involved Hatfield's wife, Antoinette. To supplement the Senator's income, she had taken up real estate sales and some home redecorating back in Washington, D.C. Basil Tsakos was a wealthy Greek national who had had some underworld connections and at that time was proposing to construct an oil pipeline across North Africa to bring Middle East oil to the West and circumvent any potential disruption of delivery via the sea lanes. He had interested Sen. Hatfield in the idea, and Hatfield had written a supportive letter on Tsakos' behalf, on Senate stationery. Meanwhile, Antoinette had contracted to redecorate Tsakos' Washington, D.C., apartment to the tune of some $60,000! The story was finally broken by The Washington Post, and the Hatfields claimed innocence but finally contributed the money to charity. The Senate Ethics Committee investigated and Hatfield was punished with a reprimand.

But the real story was the fact that the whole world knew about it *months* before The Oregonian printed a word of it, and only then when the smell reached gagging proportions. Like most newspapers of record, The Oregonian has always prided itself on its thorough coverage. For several years, they ran a promotional slogan, "If it's important to Oregonians, you'll find it in The Oregonian." But their virtual cover up of the Hatfield scandal prompted some grassroots, press-watchdog group to come up with an alternative bumper sticker, "If it's important to Oregonians, you'll find it in the The Washington Post".

I learned about myself in those focus groups, too. "Lonsdale, who's he?" "Oh, the rich guy from Bend." "Is he a Democrat or a Republican?" "Some sort of high tech guy I believe." "Dunno much about him." "But I'm ready for a change. Washington's too damn corrupt. They stay back there too long."

I needed a shot in the arm after The Oregonian poll showed us infinitely far behind, and the focus groups gave me that lift. I decided to spend even more of my own money.

# # #

For a change of pace, I went on a number of radio call-in shows. Every town of any size in the country now has these shows. They attract a large listening audience, which means the stations can charge more for their commercials. Small-town radio stations are a kick. Frequently, one person does the whole thing: plays the music, plugs in the commercial tapes, switches over to a feed from a weather service or a national news service, interviews the guest to start the ball rolling, and takes the incoming calls. These people are quick on their feet and widely, if superficially, informed on the issues, even in the smallest towns.

I was usually on over the lunch hour. What I hadn't realized, initially, was that my hour immediately followed a full hour or sometimes three solid hours of Rush Limbaugh! Now, in my book, Rush really is so right-wing that he's dangerous. His strength, of course, is that he's witty, entertaining, comes off as well informed, although his information is frequently faulty, and he knows all the hot buttons and how to push them. To 12 to 15 million "dittoheads" who tune in every day, he's the king. The king of invective and hate!

And so when I came on the air, who's out there listening but Rush's legions. They tended to be retired, white males who are universally angry about something, especially angry about our government. And why wouldn't they be, after listening to Rush day in and day out! These guys were just laying for me. In small-town Oregon, many of them were ex-loggers. I thought there was a airwaves code about the "seven naughty words" that won't be spoken on the radio. The code didn't seem to apply to our callers, especially as they referred to *me*. There were gun nuts, homophobes, Nazis, militiamen, sexists, racists, born-again Christians — sometimes all of the above, rolled up into one tortured soul — just waiting to pounce on me. They beat up on me pretty good, and there was only rarely the brave caller who defended me. (Where was that heroic kid from Boys State?)

On some call-in shows, I followed the G. Gordon Liddy show instead of Rush. It was the same result.

After a while, I'd had enough, and I refused to do call-ins if I would have followed any of the ultra-right-wing knuckleheads. But they're out there.

Not every radio station was like that, of course. Portland had several liberal stations with call-ins that were a delight to visit. And Eugene had one and, naturally, Ashland. But the good ones were badly outnumbered.

# # #

Harry Lonsdale

The Senate campaign began in earnest after Labor Day. Try as we might, prior to Labor Day people's interests were on a host of things other than a Senate race. Those few political junkies that even thought about it much weren't very turned on by a race that seemed to be decided in favor of the incumbent as early as August.

But Karen Olick wouldn't let our spirits flag, no matter how much her own may have secretly sagged. Among her other qualities, she's one of the hardest working people I've ever known. Maybe only my own father could compare with her as a workaholic. And she did her best to squeeze every last ounce of energy out of me each day.

The routine didn't change; it was the same old stuff: first and foremost, fund-raising calls, two, three, four hours a day, six days a week (only Saturday was excluded— nobody was home!); Rotary luncheons, Lions breakfasts; answering mail, thanking literally *thousands* of people who helped in one way or another; fund raisers in people's homes as many evenings as we could; meeting with groups; press conferences (when anyone from the press showed up!); meeting with the editorial boards of most of Oregon's daily newspapers, plus a few of the weeklies; radio call-in shows (only the pleasant ones); reading two or three newspapers every day and trying to watch the evening TV news, to stay current; writing checks(!); and traveling up and down Oregon's two Interstates, plus most of the state's back roads.

One of the genuine pleasures of those hectic days was reading my daily mail. I received hundreds and hundreds of letters from people all across the state, most of whom I didn't know. There were a few crank letters, to be sure, but the vast majority were supportive and beyond supportive. Those letters are among my most treasured possessions. Some were tear-jerkers, like a few from widows in their 80s, living on $400 a month Social Security, with a $25 check enclosed so that I could "go to Washington and save the trees". The way I feel about those letters was once expressed by John Steinbeck so much more poignantly than I can. In writing to a friend to thank him for the warm letter he had received, Steinbeck referred to other treasured letters he had received over the years. One from Franklin Roosevelt, another from General "Hap" Arnold of World War II fame, and then one "from a Danish bookseller telling of a woman who rowed a boat in from one of the outer islands to trade two chickens for one of my books. Those aren't very many but they are very good to have, and they bridge the times when self-love is at low ebb." ("Steinbeck. A Life in Letters." Viking Press, 1975).

But the big change that took place after Labor Day was that we started running our 30-second spots on TV, statewide. We only had two in production at that time, an introductory ad about me, saying, among other things, "You know, I voted for Mark Hatfield in the past, too, but times have changed in Oregon..." And a second spot, shot in the forest outside Bend, that talked about the overcutting of our forests, raw log exports, and concluding with the thought that "...if the Japanese want our trees, they'll have to buy our furniture, and plywood, and finished wood products to get them." Both ads were pretty low key, both were positive.

What I found totally amazing was that they worked! All of those miles on the road, all of those luncheon speeches, all of those handshakes, all of those articles in the newspapers (not nearly as many as we tried for, of course), all of those mailings, and all the rest ... *all* of that counted for almost nothing compared with our TV ads. The polls began to close; we had a race!

There was a time in my professional career as a scientist/entrepreneur when I had occasion to get a copy of the Procter and Gamble annual report. The front cover that year was one of those fold-outs, and on the inside, when you folded it all out, were photographs of P. & G.'s major products, maybe as many as 50 or 60 of them. Now I never did much food shopping, and I've told myself that, since I don't watch much TV, I'm immune to TV ads—"they're wasting their advertising bucks on *me!*"—but I was dead wrong. I recognized fully three out of four of those products. In some cases, I even knew by heart the jingles or the five-word advertising pitch that went with some of the products. "How could this be?" I asked myself. The lesson is that none of us is immune. Those ads, repeated over and over, on the tube, on billboards, in radio commercials, in newspapers and magazines, get to almost all of us. If they didn't, P. & G. wouldn't be the world's largest advertiser. If ads didn't work, the tobacco companies wouldn't be spending $5 billion a year on them.

And our ads worked, too. We were down in the polls 63-27% in late August. But by early October, with only about a month to go till election day, we were behind only 49-43%, after running our ads for about 3 weeks, and in the absence of any Hatfield ads on TV. But those ads cost us about $100,000 a week! It's amazing how much recognition and approval you can buy for a "measly" $300,000.

With our improved poll numbers, our fund-raising efforts really took off. All those people sitting on the sidelines, or those who didn't want to offend "The Senator" by supporting his opponent, began to write checks.

When we were outrageously far behind in the polls, I typically made 50 fund-raising calls per day. And of those 50 people, perhaps one or two would write a $100 check to the campaign. Few people will contribute to a perceived loser. We never gave up, but it was mighty discouraging. I said to Karen, "I should go back to my old job at Bend Research. I can make more than $100 a day *there*." But on the day that The Oregonian reported that the polls had closed to 49-43%, I made only 18 fund-raising calls. We had some events scheduled in Eugene, and I spent most of the day on the road. But, of those 18 calls, *all 18* people wrote a check! Maybe some of those who had been sitting on the sidelines thought that by contributing to the winning candidate they would gain access after the election. For whatever reason, the dough started to roll in, most of it from Oregonians, but a surprising amount from out of state, too. Even a few PACs sent us checks, even though we had tried to make it known from the beginning that we weren't accepting PAC money. We sent their checks back.

Our new-found popularity in the polls didn't help us with the Democratic leadership of the state. We sought their endorsements to build our credibility as a candidate, and to try to energize the traditional Democratic activists to get involved. Eight-term Democratic Congressman Les AuCoin, the senior member of Oregon's congressional delegation, was nowhere to be found, regarding my race. Ditto Democratic Congressman Ron Wyden. Ditto Democratic Congressman Peter DeFazio. Former Secretary of State Barbara Roberts, with whom I felt a political kinship, was too busy with her own (ultimately successful) race for governor to be of any help to our campaign.

That left our centrist Democratic governor, Neil Goldschmidt, who had been helpful to me in the past by naming me to a couple of boards. On our fifth try, we were finally allowed to actually visit with him in his office. We came prepared with a list of things he could do for us, most important, of course, being a public endorsement, followed by doing a TV spot for us, and helping us raise money. His answers to our requests were either negative or evasive. In fact, in the end, there was Neil in a *Hatfield* spot! Goldschmidt even loaned his chief of staff, Tom Imeson, to the Hatfield campaign. Working for Goldschmidt and Hatfield didn't do Imeson any harm; he became V.P. of Pacificorp, Oregon's largest utility.

It's hard to say why the Democratic big shots wouldn't touch me. Maybe I just wasn't "one of them". I was going for an important and prestigious job, and I hadn't served my apprenticeship, hadn't waited in line, as they had. Maybe they wanted the job, too! (Congressman Wyden is now Senator Wyden, after all.)

So, the hell with them, was our attitude. With all the setbacks, at 49-43% with a month to go, this race was winnable!

We knew it. And, finally, so did Mark Hatfield. I will probably never know what went on in Hatfield's Senate office and in his Portland re-election campaign office when the polls got close. Probably a touch of panic; like so many members of the Senate, holding public office was the essence of life for Mark Hatfield. He had been at it for more than 40 years, and he had never been defeated in any election.

But, if there was panic, it was matched with determination. And Hatfield had a lot more weapons in his arsenal than we had. First and foremost was his incumbency. It's difficult to exaggerate how important incumbency is to an election campaign. When the Republicans held the majority in the Senate, from 1980 until 1986, Hatfield was chair of the Appropriations committee. That gave him the ability to bring back a lot of pork to Oregon, and he came through. Maybe not as prolific a "porker" as Senator Robert Byrd of West Virginia, but right up there among the best. And there are several buildings scattered around the state with his name on them to prove it. Every state has its pork-barrelers, of course, and even with all of Hatfield's reputed clout, Oregon taxpayers still sent more money to the federal treasury annually than they got back in federal expenditures.

But incumbency also meant the ability to raise huge sums of money for election campaigns, when needed. And he needed it now. In fact, depending on how much degradation the incumbent is willing to stand, the incumbent, especially a long-term incumbent, can raise essentially unlimited money. The sources? Well, there's the list of thousands or tens of thousands of previous contributors, for starters. Every incumbent has such a list, and they spend some time keeping it current: people die, or move, so the list has to be regularly updated.

More important than previous contributors are all the PACs. Now, I've never sat down with a lobbyist representing a PAC and asked her or him for money, so I don't know how that negotiation goes. Do they ask for something specific right on the spot, in exchange for their $1000, or $2000, or $5000 check? Or is it more subtle? "Thanks for your help in the past, Senator. We're sorry we didn't get your support on that key bill last week affecting our industry, but you've been with us many times in the past, and I'm sure you will be in the future. Don't hesitate to call on me if I can supply you with any further information on..."

Or is it even more subtle than that? Simply a wink and a nod? Or not even *that*: simply an unspoken, unacknowledged compact? I guess we'll never know, unless some long-term member of Congress, on her or his retirement, sits down and writes a tell-all book. And why *should* they?

But incumbent senators have still other sources of money. There are their fellow senators, most of whom maintain their own campaign war-chest or even their own PAC, for use in a rainy day. Several senators maxed out to Hatfield, that is, they contributed the $1000 limit allowed under FEC law. The list included Strom Thurmond, Slade Gorton, Dan Coats, Conrad Burns, Bill Cohen, Phil Graham, Connie Mack, Frank Murkowski, Ted Stevens, and John Warner, among others.

But there's still more. Long-term incumbents have their choice of political celebrities to invite to come to their home state for a fund raiser or two— plus some free press. Hatfield brought out Barbara Bush, herself more popular than her husband, the then-President, for a $200,000 fund raiser. In one evening, the Hatfield campaign raised half as much money as I was ultimately to raise *total* with 5000 phone calls and countless fund-raising events.

But money-raising-ability isn't the only unfair advantage that incumbents have—though it's an enormous one, and usually the decisive one. They also have their Senate staffs available to work on their campaigns. Now, it is patently against congressional rules to use staff for this purpose, but the stories that leak out of Congress indicate that it happens all the time, although usually covertly. When it begins to get flagrant, the staff member takes unpaid leave and joins the campaign team— paid, of course.

And incumbents also have the power of franked mail. This one is no secret any longer, but free mailings, "just to stay in touch with the constituents back home", have won more than one re-election campaign.

There's simply no end to the list of incumbent advantages: friends in high places, ready access to the media (their press releases certainly have a better chance of being published); name familiarity (Hatfield's was 98% in Oregon when we started our campaign; ours was maybe 1%); and on and on. It's no wonder that incumbent members of Congress who run for re-election win more than 90% of the time. It seems that only a juicy scandal can defeat them. (A scandal, that is, that the home-state media actually cover.)

At about that time I developed a little expression that I still find useful: there are only three ways to win a major elected office in this country: be rich, be famous, or be an incumbent. And the best of these, by far, is to be an incumbent!

Whatever the reasons, Hatfield raised a cool one million dollars in three weeks in October 1990, almost all of it from PACs. It's more than we raised total, excluding my own contributions, in ten months. A partial list of Hatfield's PAC contributions is included in Appendix A. Many of those PACs don't represent one Oregon person. Also included in the Appendix is a list of major contributors from the Oregon timber industry.

I say "Hatfield raised a million dollars" but, in fact, it may not have been the senator himself. In my fund-raising efforts, I usually made the personal contact with major donors. In Hatfield's case, his right-hand man, Gerry Frank (sometimes referred to as Oregon's third senator, in those days) may have made the contacts, or it could have been others in his campaign organization.

Equally threatening for our side, (although we didn't know it at the time) was the fact that Elaine Franklin joined the Hatfield campaign. In political circles in Oregon, Elaine was known as the Wicked Witch of the West. For many years, she served as chief of staff to Oregon's junior senator, Bob Packwood, and she served him well during his several brushes with political death— the last of which were his numerous instances of unwanted sexual advances and sexual harassment that ultimately led to his resignation from office in 1995. Franklin's methods usually boiled down to one word: attack—attack the sources, attack the press, attack the attackers.

Packwood, recognizing that fellow Republican Hatfield was in trouble, and being politically much the savvier of the two, loaned Franklin to the Hatfield campaign, a move that may well be unprecedented in Oregon political history. And Elaine did her job well.

In all of Mark Hatfield's campaigns for public office, he had a reputation for being above the political fray, never attacking his opponent, usually not even mentioning his opponent by name. It was part of what led to the Hatfield legend in Oregon of being Mr. Nice Guy. That all changed when Elaine Franklin signed on.

We found ourselves being attacked with new vigor. Actually, the attacks had begun much earlier. Back in the summer, I had received a frantic phone call from Chris Babcock, the man I had chosen to replace me as president and CEO of Bend Research, when I left the company to begin campaigning.

The panicked call concerned calls he had been receiving from the government agencies back in Washington, D.C., with whom we had research and development contracts. It seems that Senator Hatfield's office had been calling all of the agencies with whom we did business to see if he could dig up any dirt on us. "Were our reports in on time? Were we delinquent in any way? Any problems with our work? Did we use any 'political influence' to get any of our contracts? Had we ever been in any trouble with that agency?" Etc. The contracting officers back in Washington, D.C., had no idea why a U.S. Senator would call and ask all these questions about a small high tech firm in Bend. Babcock understood immediately, of course. And so did I. Fortunately, our relationship with all of those agencies was so good that they called Babcock just to keep him informed.

I wrote that "Senator Hatfield's office" made the calls. I'm not certain that it was the senator himself. We were never able to verify exactly who made the calls. But, for me, it's irrelevant even if someone made the calls for him.

In every organization that I've ever been a part of, the boss always knows what's going on. Even if he or she doesn't want to know, the news reaches the person with ultimate authority. Actually, there may be one exception to that statement. According to press reports, the office of the president of the United States, over the years, has been run such that certain actions are taken in such a way that the president *doesn't* know. That is done so that, if the action blows up into a scandal, the president can maintain believable deniability. No written records show that the president was ever informed—and maybe he wasn't— and everyone around the president is sworn to secrecy. When the poop hits the fan, the underlings take the rap. It's one of the accepted responsibilities that goes with the job. Ever since Nixon and the Watergate tapes, however, I have never believed that hypothesis, and I don't believe many Americans do either. It's one of those little white lies that we have come to accept from our government. And they *know* we don't believe it. And so I assume that the boss always knows.

It was certainly true on our end of the Senate campaign. I was involved in every hire, read every press release before it went out, and carefully reviewed every word in every one of our TV spots. I may not have invented all of it, but I was aware of all of it. I realized that when the election is over, the staff go their merry way, back to Washington, D.C., or wherever. I alone remain responsible to the voters of Oregon. Which is as it should be.

If Hatfield didn't make those calls, he was responsible for them.

Then there was the "toxic polluter" episode. Bend Research is a chemical research laboratory. Chemical research labs produce chemical wastes—not much, but some. And in wide variety. We started the company in 1975, at a time before the Oregon Department of Environmental Quality existed. Seeking advice on how to handle our wastes, we went to the organization that then had cognizance, the Oregon Department of Health. In a nutshell, they told us what to do, and we did it. They inspected us regularly as the DEQ continues to do. It is important to note that the standards for the disposal of chemical wastes have gotten progressively tighter over the years, as public concerns have risen. What was quite permissible to discharge in 1975 is not permissible today. As the regulations changed, so did our practices.

We very rarely fired anyone at Bend Research. We hired carefully, and most of our employees were happy to be earning their living in a nice town like Bend. But two employees that we *did* find it necessary to "ask to leave" apparently contacted Hatfield's office to report that we were illegally discharging toxic chemicals. I was running as the environmental candidate and there's absolutely nothing that the opponent, or the press for that matter, likes better than to find out that a candidate is a hypocrite. There's no more vile word in the politician's lexicon. That's why it's used all the time. And that's what Hatfield tried to pin on me. We later learned that a Hatfield-campaign staffer named Jim Towey contacted virtually all of our ex-employees, looking for dirt.

In 1990, the head of the Oregon DEQ was a friendly bureaucrat named Fred Hansen. One Saturday evening, as Hansen and his wife were hosting a dinner party that included some friends of mine, Hatfield called from Washington, D.C. Hansen took the call in his kitchen, and we have no way of knowing—short of hearing it from either Hatfield or Hansen—what was said.

But, within a few days, a team of inspectors appeared at Bend Research's front door to carry out an unprogrammed and unannounced inspection. Normally, such inspections are scheduled well in advance, and we weren't scheduled for one for another several months. The DEQ inspectors were there, inspecting the company, its practices, and its records till midnight! And they found nothing wrong. That word apparently got back to Hatfield who wasn't satisfied, and asked Hansen for still more information, looking for a smoking gun. A copy of his letter to Hansen, dated just 17 days prior to the November 6, 1990 election, is shown on the next page.

Hansen, incidentally, later got a major promotion and a fat raise: he became the deputy director of the Environmental Protection Agency back in Washington, D.C.

The fact is that Bend Research, in its 20+ year history, has never been cited for a single violation of any type by the Oregon Department of Health or by the Oregon DEQ. When the charges were first leveled at the company, the press had a field day with it. When the charges proved to be groundless, the story was buried on the inner pages of the newspaper, or not reported at all. Two headlines from articles in The Oregonian tell it all. On October 24 an article appeared under the headline, "HATFIELD PROMPTS DEQ TO INSPECT LONSDALE HIGH-TECH COMPANY." And then on December 14, five weeks after the election was over, came a follow-up story bearing the headline, "DEQ SAYS LONSDALE COMPANY HANDLED TOXIC WASTE PROPERLY." Years later, in fact, a good television reporter from station KVAL in Eugene, Susan Castillo (now an Oregon state senator) asked me one day, "Say, Harry, what ever became of those toxic pollution charges?" What that proved to me is that, in mudslinging, once the mud has been slung, some of it has a way of sticking, no matter how hard one tries to wash it off, and no matter how unscrupulous it may have been.

When Chris Babcock told me about Hatfield's calls to our Washington, D.C., contract monitors, my response was, "Don't bother to tell *me*, go tell The Oregonian. Call a press conference and expose the bastard!" I had the same reaction to the phony "toxic polluter" charges:

for Oregon's future

October 20, 1990

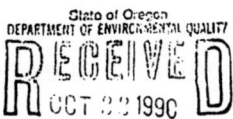

OFFICE OF THE DIRECTOR

Mr. Fred Hansen
Director
Department of Environmental Quality
Portland, Oregon 97201

Dear Mr. Hansen:

It is my understanding that the Department of Environmental Quality is conducting a hazardous waste investigation at Bend Research Company in Bend, Oregon, because of questions raised by former employees regarding the Company's toxic waste disposal methods.

I am writing to determine whether the Department of Environmental Quality conducted any soil or water tests on the premises of Bend Research during the period of April 1, 1975 until February 23, 1983. The file available to the public at your office in Bend has as its first entry a February 23, 1983, letter to DEQ from the Deschutes County Planning Department regarding a Bend Research application for a conditional use permit. Did DEQ conduct any plant inspections, toxic chemical storage inspections, hazardous waste disposal inspections, or any soil or water studies at Bend Research during those eight years and eleven months? Were any soil studies conducted at Knott's landfill during that period to determine whether toxic waste was being dumped there? And if so, what did any of these studies show?

Finally, please give me your view on whether the current investigation of Bend Research will be able to conclusively address toxic waste disposal on the premises of Bend Research and at Knott's landfill during that same period between 1975-1983.

I would appreciate your earliest possible response to these questions.

Sincerely,

Mark O. Hatfield
United States Senator

MOH:jtj

go tell the press! Sadly, he didn't. His thinking, and it's not entirely faulty, was that in a pissing contest between us and the senator, we were almost certainly going to lose—if not immediately, then later. A U.S. Senator carries an enormous amount of clout relative to that of the common citizen—much too much, in fact—and Babcock realized that there were dozens of jobs at stake in the company. If things *really* got nasty, there was a chance, he felt, that our company could be forced out of business somehow. I felt, and still feel, that that simply couldn't happen in America. Maybe I'm just naive. Babcock's reaction, instead of going to the press, was to distance the company from *me*. I received a memo asking me to "...publicly downplay my role in Bend Research". Downplay? It was my life's work!

In terms of the election campaign, the entire episode had little real impact: much smoke, no fire. But it has certainly had a long-lasting impact on my relationships with my former company and its CEO. And it raised questions in people's minds about my integrity.

Hatfield abused his power in other ways. Our favorite TV reporter throughout the campaign was Mark Hass of station KATU, the ABC affiliate in Portland. Mark didn't play "gotcha" journalism—to quote Ross Perot—as some of his peers sometimes did. He asked straight questions and put the essence of our response on the news.

But apparently Hass became too friendly toward me. One day we noticed that he wasn't covering the race anymore. A new man, Dan Christopher, got the assignment. When next I saw Hass and asked him what had happened, he said that the Senator called the station management and told them to have someone else cover the campaign. And they did. (Hass is now a member of the Oregon State Legislature and one of his principal issues is campaign finance reform.)

The editor of a small daily newspaper in Tillamook, The Headlight-Herald, a man named Carl Anderson, called me up once, late in the campaign, to tell me that Hatfield had called and told him to run a major front-page article exclusively on him, just prior to the election. He refused. Again, I suggested that he go to The Oregonian with the story. He declined. "It would be the end of my career."

Gerry Frank, Hatfield's right-hand man, got into the act, too. For years, Frank has had the additional, paid job of writing a weekly column for The Oregonian. But Frank's name was so closely associated with Hatfield's—he had worked for the Senator for almost 20 years—that we repeatedly contacted the paper and asked them to drop Frank's column for the duration of the campaign. They refused: "He's not stumping for the senator in his column; never even mentions his name." Which was true.

But then some alert staffer in our campaign noticed that Frank had a way of heaping an inordinate amount of praise on one or two individuals in his columns, and that those individuals turned out to be major Hatfield contributors! Again, we asked The Oregonian to drop the column. Again they refused. Finally, about a month before the election, Frank voluntarily suspended his column.

There was more. Joe Uris and Ted Weisback, two humorous, fast-talking, ultra-liberal disc jockeys at a leading Portland radio station, KGW, the NBC affiliate, had me on their shows regularly and allowed me to present my case. It was one of those friendly call-in shows, and I enjoyed it. They invited Hatfield to appear, too, by phone from Washington, D.C., but he regularly declined. He only did call-ins, he explained, if the questions were all screened in advance and he could select those that he wanted to respond to. Late in the campaign, we noticed that their shows had been canceled. "Word from Hatfield" was what they passed on to us. After the election, their lives didn't improve. One was living in Canada at last report; the other was still doing radio, but not in Portland.

Now, none of those abuses affected the outcome of the election in any significant way, it seems to me. But they do show how far someone with power will go to retain that power. I suspect that congressional challengers all across the country run into the same sort of buzz saw, although they may not even be aware of it. I don't know who I respect the least: the power abuser, or the person being abused who doesn't blow the whistle. Abe Lincoln once said it well: "To sin by silence when they should protest makes cowards of men."

It's been said that politics is a contact sport. That's a polite way of putting it. One thing was certain after those shenanigans: Hatfield was "No more Mr. Nice Guy" in our book.

But back to Elaine Franklin, Packwood's chief of staff who was helping Hatfield. The scary thing about having an unprincipled opponent is that you're never quite sure just what they're up to. Along with all of the respectable jobs that fall into the campaign consultant profession, there's one called "opposition research". For pay, those people will try to dig up any recorded dirt, from however far back, of whatever type, on your opponent. They will even follow them around, night and day, for pay. We were offered the services of such organizations, and declined. Somehow, we just knew that Elaine had hired one of those firms, looking for the knock-out punch.

The only times we actually saw Elaine in action was when she attended some of our fund raisers (how did she even know about them?) with pen and pad in hand, and proceeded to write down the names of our attendees. A not-so-subtle threat: "The senator won't like it if you contribute to his opponent."

# # #

So much happens in the last few weeks of a contested election campaign. That's the time when almost all of the voters—or at least a decisive fraction— make up their minds.

The late Ron Brown, who was then head of the Democratic National Committee in Washington, D.C., came to Oregon to do a fund raiser for us. Brown became President Clinton's Commerce Secretary, and the right-wing of the Republican party attacked him for several months, as a way to attack the president, before his tragic death in a plane crash in Bosnia. Brown, to me, was the consummate American: principled, hard-working, generous, and fair-minded. He was also a great stump-speaker.

Our race started drawing national attention when the polls showed it was close. Cokie Roberts of ABC News showed up at our campaign headquarters for an interview, as did Helen Dewar of The Washington Post. *Time* magazine and The New York Times gave the race some space, with headlines like "Upset in the Making?". Even the Friday-evening and Sunday-morning TV political pundits had something to say about the race. Pundit Jack Germond of the Baltimore Sun even picked me to win.

In spite of the dirty tricks campaign against us, our poll numbers stayed high. With a week to go, one poll even gave us a small lead.

For months, we had challenged Hatfield to debate us. It certainly wasn't that I was some crackerjack debater. I had never entered into a political debate in my life. But it would have been free press for us, in addition to a chance to have the two of us confront the issues: What *do* we do about the remaining forests on public lands? Does a woman have the right to choose a safe and legal abortion, or doesn't she? And what about all those campaign contributions? — weren't they corrupting the system?

Hatfield declined all of our overtures. I suppose his thinking was, "Why do I want to give this guy any spotlight?" His formal response to the press inquiries was, "I won't have this campaign made into a circus. I'll stand on my record!" It worked. We never debated.

But the City Club of Portland, the state's leading producer of notable out-of-town speakers, debates, and issue discussion, put on a one-chair debate, which is their practice when one of the debate invitees declines. It went well for our side, as expected. What stole the show, though, was a thick pile of computer print-outs that I lugged up onto the stage with me. It was a record of all of Hatfield's PAC contributors, direct from the Federal Election Commission. There were hundreds of them, mostly from out-of-state organizations that were looking for something in return. (There's an abbreviated list in Appendix A.)

With only a few days to go before the election, the staff concocted a clever but desperate scheme. Hatfield was holding a press conference the next day, and I was to crash it and, with the TV cameras rolling, again publicly challenge him to a debate. Even if he declined, that fact at least would make the evening news. We did it, even though it exhibited more boldness than is really in me. When Hatfield approached the small press room at the Portland Hilton hotel with his contingent of people, I was waiting in the hall, and stuck out my hand to shake his. He didn't immediately recognize me — we had only actually met in person twice in the entire multi-month campaign — and he took my hand. Then, when he realized who I was, he wrenched his hand from mine as though he had been shaking hands with a cobra. His press conference was a disaster. I was standing there the whole time and when he attacked me by name he became flummoxed and stumbled badly. I made my challenge when he opened the press conference up to questions. He didn't even respond, but instead stormed out of the room, with his contingent trailing. It was fun, and it made the evening news, but it was inconsequential to the bottom line.

# # #

I'm ashamed to admit how scared I was throughout the campaign, almost on a daily basis. Even after several months, campaigning was still a foreign land for me. Mostly, it was fear of the unknown. Once in a while, you met with familiar people, even friends. But almost every day it was something or someone new. And I'm a failure at remembering names. "I'm sorry, tell me your name again. ... er, again?"

The drive from Portland to Eugene down Interstate 5 takes about two hours, a little less if you're in a hurry. It's beautiful farmland almost the entire way. About five miles out from Eugene, there's a precipice that comes down to the highway on the east side. It became my signal: "Ye gods, I'm *on* in about ten minutes. Let's see, what am I going to say again? Will there be TV cameras? Friendly crowd?" There was that feeling in the pit of my stomach. Dry mouth started all over again. Multiply that by maybe six to eight times a day, 200 days in a row, and you get the picture. It's just part of the entry fee.

I had started to count the days until the election back in the late winter, when there were still almost 300 days to go. By the last three weeks, I was counting hours. I wanted it over, win or lose. Campaigning, for me, was like wearing one of those shirts that is tight around the collar, and it has one of those chafing labels that gets you right in the back of the neck. You can't wait to take the shirt off and cut out that goddam label.

# # #

We made a lot of mistakes along the way. None of them cost us the election, but there were some things I wish we hadn't done.

Here's one. Gerry Frank, Hatfield's chief of staff in the Senate, in addition to writing a column for The Oregonian, also wrote travel books. His book, *Dining Out in New York*, reputedly is *the* best seller on the subject. Of course, he had to travel to all the places he wrote about in his books, and it seems that he frequently did the travel as part of some Senate business. But Dan Walter, our press secretary, did some checking on his own—maybe because we were mad at Frank for his newspaper column—and discovered an inordinate number of trips, paid for by the U.S. Government. And then Dan went too far and reported it to the press without my seeing the press release, and the press printed a story about it.

It was dumb. I learned about it the evening that Dan reported it to the press. I was furious, and chewed him out, big time. If Gerry Frank were cheating on his travel, it was Uncle Sam's business, not ours. Our target was Hatfield, not Frank. Much later, much too late, I wrote Gerry Frank an apology letter. He accepted it gracefully but he and I both knew that mud, once slung, never completely comes off.

# # #

We had one final ignominy to deal with. Just a few weeks before the election, a group of prominent Democrats, led by then-Portland City Councilman Earl Blumenauer and a former friend of mine, Elizabeth Furse, started a petition drive called Democrats for Hatfield. Several dozen of Oregon's better known Democrats signed on, and the list, and their message supporting Hatfield, was sent to hundreds of thousands of Oregon households. I believe that it was John F. Kennedy who said, "Forgive your enemies, but remember their names." Blumenauer, incidentally, is now *Congressman* Blumenauer, from Oregon's Third Congressional District and Furse became *Congresswoman* Furse, from Oregon's First Congressional District.

# # #

The home stretch. If we carried out focus groups to look for Hatfield's vulnerabilities, the Hatfield-Elaine Franklin team was certain to have done so on me. Inevitably, they found something. In the early 1980s, a guru from India who went by the name of Bhagwan Shree Rajneesh settled with his commune in central Oregon. They chose a 160,000-acre, very remote spot on which to build their small town, a town that became known as Rajneeshpuram. They immediately became controversial. First, they were mostly non-Oregonians; in fact, many of them were Europeans or Asians. Second, they lived a very unconventional life-style, as all communes seem to do. They grew almost all their own food, wore robes of an identical color, engaged in free sex (it was said), and, religiously, were free thinkers. Eventually the commune swelled to almost 5000 people, but from day one, their relations with their neighbors got increasingly threatening. This in spite of the fact that the nearest town, Antelope, population 50, was 27 miles away.

And the press reports were invariably bad. Whatever the commune's intentions, they found no supporters among the Oregon establishment. To some of us, it seemed that their main desire was to be left alone.

Curious, I once drove the 90 miles from Bend to see for myself. What I found wasn't what I was reading in the newspapers at all. I found easygoing, harmless, well-educated people trying to find a new and unconventional way of living. Before the commune was finally abandoned in the late '80s I made three day-trips there, just talking with the folks.

The followers may have been gentle, but some of the leaders and particularly a woman named Ma Anand Sheela were ruthless. Eventually, the mutual enmity between the commune and their neighbors got out of control. Some crimes were committed by followers of the Bhagwan, and he fled east in a chartered airplane. He was apprehended in North Carolina, apparently on his way to Bermuda, and brought back to Oregon in chains. He was ultimately convicted of having performed illegal marriages, and forced to leave the country. (He has since died, in India.)

My experience with the people I'd met at the commune had been positive, and I wanted to defend them because I had never seen such one-sided, inflammatory treatment of any group by the press. I wrote an opinion piece and bought a display ad for it in The (Bend) Bulletin newspaper. The full ad, from November 21, 1985, is shown on the next page. A couple of folks called to thank me for speaking out, but mostly there was silence. My response was heartfelt, but politically naive.

Polls later showed that the Bhagwan and his commune and their doings drove Oregonians nuts. It was the single most explosive and divisive issue in Oregon in the 1980s. The Hatfield camp used the issue to discredit me relentlessly and with great success. All that money raised from all those PACs was now used in a TV bombardment. The ads depicted me as a Bhagwan follower (I had never met the man, of course), and there were unflattering split-screen visuals of him and me, side by side. In my hometown of Bend, there were Bhagwan ads run against me every hour on the hour, along with other attack ads, for the last couple of weeks of the campaign. We ran no attack ads in our campaign.

Running
Politics, Power, and the Press

Goodbye, Bhagwan

Well, he's gone. And a lot of folks are relieved.

But his sudden departure leaves a lot of questions unanswered. Was he really running away to Bermuda to avoid prosecution? (Don't we have an extradition agreement with Bermuda?) And was he really guilty of crimes, or just disgusted with a country that would chain and manacle an innocent-until-proven-guilty human being and haul him from jail to jail for 10 days without allowing him bail? We may never know the answers to these and other questions. Will any of the so-called investigative reporters be able to get the answers, or have they sufficiently alienated themselves from the Rajneeshees to preclude them from ever getting the full story?

The Bhagwan said "There is no God," and most people didn't want to hear that. He preached free love, and most people didn't want to hear that either (although a flock of folks secretly engage in promiscuity and extra-marital relationships). Some of us feel that he was railroaded out of the country, in a movement spearheaded by bigots, religious and otherwise. Most of our government leaders, both elected and those-who-would-be-elected, made political cannon-fodder out of him. And one can't overlook the decisive role played by the media. The newpapers and TV shaped the opinion of most of us. How many of those who opposed the Bhagwan ever actually visited Rajneeshpuram to observe that vibrant, happy town of 3000 intelligent people living off the land?

Sometimes it's hard to remember that the Pilgrims came to America to escape religious intolerance. The legacy they've given us is that we have religious freedom only as long as we do it the Anglo-Saxon, Christian way. Maybe this was one time when the silent majority — those who rightly felt that the Bhagwan wasn't hurting anyone and should have been left alone — shouldn't have remained so silent.

The harassment and abuse heaped on this gentle man is something that all of us, as freedom-loving Americans, can be ashamed of. We can't help but wonder what might have happened if, like many spiritual leaders before him, the Bhagwan had not pleaded guilty and run away but had stood his ground and suffered the consequences.

Harry Lonsdale

A-8   THE BULLETIN

The newspapers, too, had their say. There are 18 daily newspapers in Oregon, and dozens that publish less frequently. Of all the dailies, every one endorsed Hatfield. The Oregonian, in their endorsing editorial, said "it would be an act of political self-mutilation not to elect Hatfield". The main reason for their endorsement was his clout, his ability to bring home the bacon for Oregon. The fact that, even if all the nice things they said about him were true (and there was scant mention of his prior ethical problems), no one pointed out that he had to leave office *some* day, no matter what, and what about the loss of clout *then*? Could Oregon survive such a cataclysm? (He has since left, and the state has somehow survived.)

I was endorsed by only one newspaper, The (Sisters) Nugget, a free weekly with a distribution of 6000.

# # #

With maybe 100 hours to go before the election, I got to thinking of what it would be like if I won. I had had similar visions of that outcome before, but now it seemed particularly real. What kind of a senator would I be? What kind of staff would I hire? What would be my first, or my first three, main issues? What would it take to save the public forests? Could one senator from a Western state bring it off?

Would I become one of "them"? Who could I form effective coalitions with? Would I be marginalized because I was too pushy, too uncompromising on my key issues?

Like most Americans, I had ambivalent feelings about members of Congress. On some issues, some of them seemed like heroes, with the wisdom of Solomon. But then I thought of all the deal-making, the PACs, the money-in-politics, the gamesmanship, the double-talk. I decided there was only one way to play it: straightforwardly. And if I became marginalized because of it? So be it. But didn't every freshman go back there with exactly this set of principles? What happened to them? Was I any better?

All unanswerable questions. But I made one specific commitment: I was taking the litter-cleanup campaign back to Washington, D.C., with me. Every Earth Day, I and whatever other Senators I could talk into joining me were putting on our old clothes and cleaning up our nation's capital. A small matter, to be sure, but one where the bully pulpit that goes with the job could be put to good use.

# # #

On the eve of election day, four of us piled into my car, now with 45,000 miles of campaign experience on it, and drove around the state for 24 hours. It was a campaign stunt, pure and simple. We weren't looking for that last hand to shake—that was still to come—we were looking for press coverage on election day. Lawton Chiles, who became governor of

Florida, once walked the entire length of his state when he was running for the Senate. He won. And George McGovern, in his unsuccessful run for the presidency, once walked the width of Iowa. He lost.

The drive-a-thon was fun. We stopped everywhere we thought there might be a photo-op: a late night bowling alley, a small-town hospital at 3 a.m., a logger's diner at 5 a.m.

We arrived back in Portland late on election day, Tuesday, Nov. 6, 1990. I had already voted absentee, so my last remaining job was to ... shake more hands! I went to a couple of polling places to greet folks on their way to vote.

A race that had had its zanier moments couldn't have ended on a more appropriate note. At 7:55 p.m., that is, exactly *five minutes* before the polls closed, on a chilly, drizzly evening, I'm shaking the last hand, a man in his 40s, in northeast Portland. I did my usual, "Hi, I'm Harry Lonsdale. I'd appreciate your vote today." His response? "Oh, so you're Harry Lonsdale. I think I'll vote for you." And maybe he did.

# # #

There are few things as final as the conclusion to an election campaign. One minute you're running your ass off. A minute later, the polls close, and there's absolutely nothing left to do.

We went back to our campaign headquarters to drink beer and await the results. A crowd began to form, old friends, new friends, supporters, volunteers, hangers-on, the press.

The results weren't long in coming in. By 11 p.m. the result was clear: Hatfield 53.6%, Lonsdale 46.4%.

We had lost.

CHAPTER 3.

IF AT FIRST YOU DON'T SUCCEED

It's hard to lose, very hard. The humiliation, loss of face, all those volunteer hours, all the speeches, highway miles, down the drain. The feeling of REJECTION!

When I thought about it rationally, I drew comfort from the fact that more than half a million Oregonians voted for me over Mark Hatfield, the darling of the Oregon press corps, the man who had never lost an election (and has now retired, still undefeated). 46% of the voters had chosen *me*, a man they hadn't even heard of just 6 months prior to election day. Occasionally, during my grieving period, I'd ask myself, "So how did I do so *well*?!"

And there were all those hundreds of letters of condolence. "We were proud to have voted for you" ... "took a lot of guts" ... "go do it again!..." I even received personal letters from politicians from around the country, most of whom I didn't even know. Bill Clinton and Al Gore — neither one exactly a household name in 1990 — wrote notes, Clinton telling me how he felt when he lost his first re-election campaign for Arkansas governor. Joe Lieberman, Democratic Senator from Connecticut (and the 2000 candidate for vice president), whom I had met and came to admire, told me how he felt when he lost his first race for the U.S. House: "You walk around in a daze for a few days... ."

It was an especially difficult time for me, because my mother died less than a month after the election. She had suffered from congestive heart failure during the final stages of the campaign, and I feel certain that her passing was not unrelated to my losing. My mom and I were about as close as a mother and son can be. It was a terrible loss.

But the mind, as well as the body, has a way of healing. And all those fan letters definitely helped.

Still pretty innocent about things political, it took me some months to realize that what I had done, and the time and personal money I had invested, didn't have to be money down the drain. I had built up that intangible commodity called name identification.

Ask yourself who you voted for for governor in the last election. And why did you vote for that person? Maybe it was simply because he or she was the Democrat (Republican) on the ballot, and you're a regular Democratic (Republican) voter. More likely, you had heard of the candidate on the evening news because of something they had done, in politics or out. Or maybe you knew of that person because he/she had previously held some lesser elected job. Somehow, some way, you had heard about that person, probably in a favorable way.

Steve Largent, ex-football star, serves in the U.S. House of Representatives, as did TV star Sonny Bono until his untimely death in late 1997. And when Sonny died, who did the Republican Party press to run in his place? Why his widow, Mary, of course. Is she qualified? you ask. The answer is, it doesn't matter. She has the Bono name, a name known all across America and throughout California's 44th Congressional District. The only *real* question was, did she *want* the job? Her answer was "yes", which immediately made her the front-runner for the job, and she won the seat handily in a special election. (About her qualifications for office, let me add this: for my money, *of course* she's qualified. I believe in a citizen legislature.)

So there I was, with a million-plus dollars already invested in name I.D., a fine group of supporters, and a list of contributors from all across Oregon. Why not try again? In addition to wanting to save forests, I now had even stronger convictions about the need for campaign finance reform after my battle with Hatfield and his avalanche of money. Bob Packwood, Oregon's junior senator, already finishing his fourth 6-year term, was up for re-election in 1992. He wasn't the principal perpetrator of national forest destruction that Hatfield was. But he was no friend of the environment and a big friend of the timber industry in Oregon, and was well entrenched with most of the Republican establishment. He was one more career politician, a master fund-raiser with a contributor list, rumor had it, cultivated over two decades and 60,000 names long! He was also Oregon's "PAC master", raking in more PAC money every election cycle than the rest of the Oregon congressional delegation combined.

Packwood was a politician who made no bones, nor moral judgments, about doing deals for his constituents, whoever they happened to be that year: timber companies, the cable TV industry, bankers, whatever. When the Republicans had control of the Senate from 1980 to 1986, Packwood was chair of the Finance Committee—where he had virtually unlimited ability to raise campaign contributions—and still in 1992 he was ranking minority member. Barlett and Steele, in their wonderful exposé of how Congress works, "America. Who Pays the Taxes?", talk about how Packwood crowed about walking around the Senate floor as the 1986 Tax Reform Act was taking shape, with fellow senators jamming little slips of paper in his jacket pockets indicating the price of their votes: special arcane provisions inserted into the bill to benefit their cash constituents back home. Packwood once even described himself as a "whore", but I suppose he'd say he was a loyal whore. It was said of his support that it was a mile wide and an inch deep. He lived in Washington D.C., only traveling back to Oregon to campaign, raise money, get some free press, and "show the colors". He maintained no residence in Oregon.

So there I was in the summer of 1991, trying again to decide whether to run for the U.S. Senate. I found myself going through the same gyrations and mood swings I had experienced prior to the Hatfield race. I remember thinking, "Not those fucking, degrading phone calls for money again! *Anything* but that! And those press bastards: just laying for me again, no doubt." Actually, on election night 1990, the first question the press corps threw at me after my concession speech was would I run again? (They knew the shtick better than I did.) "Nope, not for me," was my reply. "Let someone else try it next time." And so, if I decided to try again, my first press conference would be devoted to tactfully eating those words.

I applied the same three-day rule to myself as I had used in 1990: if I felt the same way about running, pro or con, three days in a row, I'd go with that decision. It was several weeks before three-days-in-a-row happened.

I was helped along with my decision by the fact that nine-term Democratic Congressman Les AuCoin, from Oregon's First District, had announced in the spring of '92 that he was challenging Packwood. Now, for me, it became a "twofer". AuCoin was one more career politician, who seemed to lack an ethical compass but knew how to raise money and get re-elected. He sat on the House Appropriations Committee—the cash cow of the committees—and in his position on the Interior subcommittee of Appropriations he was able to inflict a lot of damage on Oregon's national forests. While less powerful than Hatfield, his penchant for "getting the cut out" on the forests wasn't less effective than Hatfield's for lack of effort. During Appropriation Committee hearings on the Forest Service budget one year, Les in no uncertain terms told the then-chief of the USFS that it was "the cut or his job". The chief got the message. Like almost all multi-term members of Congress, AuCoin had built up a war chest of unused campaign funds from his previous election campaigns: more than half a million dollars worth. He'd need a lot more — and must have felt he could raise it — to compete with Bob Packwood, who was a consummate fund-raiser.

While the Hatfield campaign had depleted my personal financial resources, I still wasn't broke, and I felt that, if I chose to run, I'd have at least a running start, again with my own money, and if those 5000 contributors from '90 would only come through again, ...

Serendipity played a part. In the midst of my indecision, a mutual acquaintance invited me to have that meeting I mentioned earlier with former President Jimmy Carter. The acquaintance ran a fishing lodge in Ft. Klamath, Oregon, and Carter had stayed there before and used it as a base for some local fly-fishing on the Williamson River. Carter, with his wife, Rosalynn, was staying at the lodge in the summer of '91, and I was invited to join them over a simple streamside lunch.

The setting: a beautiful day, a few folding chairs, card tables with some Wonder Bread sandwiches, and some cold pop. About midday, the presidential couple, decked in fishing gear, came around the bend in their guided driftboat. We were there to greet them.

I've long been a Carter fan. As I look back on the presidents of my lifetime, beginning with FDR, it seems to me that one man stands out in honor and integrity. We ask a lot of our presidents, as well we should. We want them to keep us out of wars, to raise our standard of living, curb inflation, to not increase the national debt, to keep the Interstate highways paved and, for some of us, to keep those Social Security checks coming on time. But that's not all. We want the president to be our *moral* leader as well. And it's on that score that most of our leaders of the second half of this century have failed. Except for Jimmy Carter, scandals have swirled around our presidents either during their lifetimes or posthumously.

Carter drew some tough breaks as president: roaring inflation and soaring interest rates, perhaps because he didn't kowtow to the gnomes of Wall St.; and then the Iran hostage mess and the failed rescue attempt. He is probably unchallenged as the best *ex*-president we've ever had, with his ongoing crusades for world peace, against disease, and to help the homeless. I've often wondered what the country would be like today if he had defeated Ronald Reagan in 1980 and won a second term.

I had some political questions I wanted to ask him, but, even more importantly, I wanted to see him as a human being. He struck me as sincere, bright, honest, forthright, patriotic, concerned for his country (even on a fishing outing), and down-to-earth — even a bit shy, I thought. Not humble, exactly, but warm and genuine.

My burning question for President Carter was this: could one senator make a difference? Could I, for example, in coalition with others, save what was left of the national forests? His response, "In time, yes. Probably within one six-year term." Could I clean up campaign finance? "That's much tougher." But he felt that I could make a start, as an insider, if I remained true to my principles — as he had.

We only had an hour together, and then he and Rosalynn climbed back into the boat and drifted on downstream. I haven't forgotten that meeting.

# # #

Feeling that I could really make a difference, I was a step closer to running. It took one more event to put me over the top. Ask any American what is the deepest canyon in the U.S. and virtually every one of them will say, "the Grand Canyon." And, at a mile deep and spectacularly beautiful, that's not a bad guess. But it's wrong. Most people from Idaho and Oregon know that the deepest canyon in North America, and one of the deepest and most spectacular in the world, is Hell's Canyon, which forms much of the border between Idaho and Oregon. It's 6000 feet deep, sometimes snow-covered at the top when it's 80°F at the bottom, and it's one of the most remote areas in the lower 48.

A good friend, Ric Bailey, called me one day in the summer of 1991 to invite me on a float trip through Hell's Canyon. Ric is a float-trip guide, a strong and courageous environmentalist. This wasn't your run-of-the-mill float trip. Ric had lined up some of the best people of the national environmental movement: members of most of the national and state groups who spent their working days trying to protect unique places like Hell's Canyon. As a special treat, Ric had invited his friend and Hell's

Canyon supporter singer Carole King on the trip, and she brought her guitar.

My date for the trip was Portlander Mitzi Scott, who had labored hard on the '90 campaign and had become more than a good friend. This was a 4-day trip through roaring rapids, eye-popping scenery, and all of the outdoor life you could ask for. Mitzi and I talked about politics off and on during the entire trip. Mitzi knew, as few do, just how corrupt and money-driven modern politics can be. Like me, she had no love lost for *any* career politician, Democrat or Republican. In 1990, she had chaired Oregon Governor Neil Goldschmidt's re-election campaign before Neil dropped out, citing personal reasons. Except for Neil—and me—she had trouble finding candidates to believe in, who ran for the right reasons. She knew full well that both Les AuCoin, in the primary, and Bob Packwood, in the general, would be formidable, well-financed opponents. All the more reason to knock 'em off, was her attitude. As for me, I was still straddling the fence, still a bit wounded and a lot angry.

Toward the end of the trip, out of the blue Mitzi blurted out, "So, are you just going to let Les and Bob get away with it?!" Sometimes just a few words, if they're the right words, can turn your life around. And those were the right words for me at that moment.

I didn't realize it until I woke up the next morning, but I was committed. "Aw, shit," I thought, "here we go all over again!"

# # #

There's not much about campaigning for elected office that I haven't already described. At least this time I knew where to start: hire the best staff I could find, starting with an experienced campaign manager and a good press secretary. I even knew where to look: the job bank at the Democratic Senatorial Campaign Committee. Karen Olick wasn't available to me, unfortunately, as she was already committed to Barbara Boxer's U.S. Senate campaign in California (Boxer won; Karen became her chief of staff.) I found a very capable manager in Cynthia Wieland, who had experience running congressional campaigns. And Cynthia found a first-rate press secretary in Kathy McShea (who, until recently, served as press secretary to Senator Carl Levin of Michigan). Mitzi agreed to get involved in fund raising, as did Kris Rees, who had helped with the '90 campaign. Also from the first campaign, Joe Trippi signed on to do the media work, and Paul Maslin again agreed to do the polling. And, in a matter of a few weeks, we had an experienced team assembled. "On the road again ... ."

Adlai Stevenson ran for president twice, in 1952 and 1956, each time hopelessly overmatched by Dwight Eisenhower. But Stevenson did us all the favor of writing down some of his experiences in his book, "Major Campaign Speeches, 1952," (Random House, 1953), and elsewhere. Here's what he had to say about a typical day of campaigning:

"You must emerge, bright and bubbling with wisdom and well-being, every morning at 8 o'clock, just in time for a charming and profound breakfast talk, shake hands with hundreds, often literally thousands of people, make several inspiring, 'newsworthy' speeches during the day, confer with political leaders along the way and with your staff all the time, write at every chance, think if possible, read mail and newspapers, talk on the telephone, talk to everybody ... Then, all you have to do is make a great, imperishable speech, get out through the pressing crowds, ... your hand bruised, and back to the hotel—in time to see a few important people.

"But the real work has just commenced—two or three or sometimes four hours of frenzied writing and editing of the next day's immortal mouthings so you can get something ... to the reporters so they can get something to their newspapers by deadline time ... Finally, sleep, sweet sleep, steals you away, unless you worry—which I do..."

The way Stevenson described it, campaigning can actually be fun—tiring, but fun. But he ran in the days before TV was everything, back when the two political parties picked the candidates in smoke-filled rooms,—but when the parties also *funded* the candidates. So, while there's a lot of commonality between a 1952 campaign and a 1992 campaign, what was missing from his daily log was *fund-raising calls*: a minimum of three to four hours worth, every day. Without those ugly and demeaning fund-raising calls, I imagine that campaigning could actually be *fun*. Another major difference between then and now is that when Stevenson gave a speech, a) people showed up to hear it, and b) the press covered it. Nowadays, cynicism and TV-addiction are so pervasive that very few people even show up for political rallies anymore. The press, if they show up at all, frequently ignores what the candidate *says* and reports instead on some peccadillo-of-the-day. And the people, the voters that the candidate is trying so desperately to reach, expect to be hand-fed through their television set!

# # #

One of my first chores was to call Les AuCoin and tell him that I was in the race. He was gracious, initially trying to talk me out of it but then seeing that that was fruitless, wishing me well and promising a clean, issues-oriented campaign.

Ha!

Some weeks later, a third candidate named Joe Wetzel, a Portland lawyer, entered the Democratic primary. It was rumored, and Joe confirmed it to me over lunch one day, that he had no personal money to put into the race—*ergo*, I knew even more certainly than he did that he couldn't possibly win the primary election. But I also knew that "Wetzel votes" were votes for the outsider, that is, votes taken away from *me*. Politically, Joe, who was a nice guy, good family man, and devout Catholic, was miles to the right of me. He was very much pro-life, he wanted to *increase* the timber cut on federal lands, etc. Still, I had a lot of sympathy for Joe. In many ways, he was like me: fed up with the system, seeking a voice, and willing to put up with all the crap, the press-bashing, and perhaps the ugliest cut of all—being ignored—because he had some principles that he wanted to stand up for. I admired him, and still do.

We had some new faces on the campaign staff, but, at heart, they were very much like the '90 staff: young, intelligent, high energy, principled. And we set up our headquarters back in our old digs, across the street from the county library in downtown Portland. The grind, unfortunately, was the same: fund-raising calls every morning; barreling north and south on I-5 and east and west on I-84, eventually again reaching every town in Oregon; meetings with newspaper editors; talks at Rotaries, Chambers, Lions; "houseparties" (a.k.a. fund raisers); cutting TV spots; doing radio "feeds"; answering mail; DRIVING.

Something I had wanted to do in the '90 campaign but never found time for, was writing down a comprehensive yet succinct summary of my positions on the issues of the day. It turned into an eight-page, 11 X 17" pamphlet that Mitzi Scott dubbed "A Blueprint for Change". In the background on the cover page was part of a page of the blueprints from the Portland home that Mitzi was building at the time. We tried to cover it all: the economy, the environment, energy, universal health care, education, labor, drugs and crime, defense and foreign policy, human rights, and (my favorite) honest government and campaign finance reform. We mailed out 10,000 copies, including copies to the press. No longer could the press call me a one-issue candidate, as they had in the '90 campaign.

One enormous difference between '90 and '92 was press coverage. We couldn't *buy* any in '90. But now that I had name I.D., the press covered our stuff. AuCoin had a clever and aggressive press secretary who knew how to get his stuff into print too. Besides, AuCoin was very well known in Portland, part of which was in his congressional district. Most of the time it seemed that we were on the defensive, answering AuCoin's attacks. But, hey, *any* press was better than *no* press.

We made the obligatory chase for endorsements, but with little success. I felt certain that we'd win the NARAL endorsement, considering that Kate Michelman, their executive director, had come to Oregon twice to campaign for me in '90. But AuCoin was solidly pro-choice, too. We were both in for a comeuppance: NARAL endorsed Bob Packwood even before the primary! I visited Michelman in Washington, D.C., and gave her a bad time about it, but to no avail. Packwood was a NARAL and pro-choice advocate even back when it was considered unpopular.

AuCoin was good on labor issues and he easily won the AFL-CIO endorsement for the primary. They obviously hadn't forgotten my ill-considered "...American workers are overpaid..." statement of a decade earlier. But the deepest cut of all came from my environmentalist buddies. I *knew* I could count on their endorsement. But it was not to be. The Oregon League of Conservation Voters, representing all of the major enviro. groups in Oregon, did a "no endorsement" between AuCoin and me. "We know he's bad on forest issues, Harry, but he's 100% on everything else on our list." Yeah, he's great on stuff 500 miles or more away from Oregon!

# # #

One thing hadn't changed from '90: right from the beginning we were behind in the polls. In the poll that mattered, only registered Democratic voters were included. In that group, AuCoin was pretty popular and well known, at least in the Portland metro area, which represented almost half of the Dems. in Oregon. However, when a cross-section of *all* voters was surveyed, both AuCoin and I were ahead of Packwood, and I did even better against Packwood than AuCoin did.

This time, finally, we had debates: three of them, in Grants Pass, a down-state timber town; in Portland; and in Pendleton, in eastern Oregon wheat-country. I was really looking forward to those debates. I had never debated in public before in my life, but there was plenty I wanted to say about the state of politics in our country, and public debates were the best place imaginable to get my thoughts on record—and against someone who represented that sorry state of politics. I felt that we would get plenty of press coverage and perhaps even gavel-to-gavel TV coverage.

We held a couple of debate-prep sessions, in which I was grilled by some of the sharpest political minds we could find in Oregon. Those folks were merciless. Not only did they throw at me every tough political question on the '90s agenda, they threw in some highly personal stuff, including a few things that they knew were totally slanderous fabrications, just to see how I'd handle them.

But, whatever they did, it didn't toughen me up enough. The first debate was held at Rogue Community College in Grants Pass, in front of a packed house. The format for the debates was established by the Oregon League of Women Voters, which presumably uses a format recommended by the national League. It goes like this: Candidate A has 30 seconds to ask a question of Candidate B. Candidate B then has 60 seconds to respond. And then Candidate A has 30 additional seconds in which to rebut. Then it's Candidate B's turn to ask a question, and so on.

After our introductory statements, AuCoin led off the candidate questions. His very first question floored me. (I give him credit; he had obviously been through debates before, and knew some good tricks.) AuCoin's first "question" went something like this: "Harry, as a multimillionaire who's trying to buy a seat in the U.S. Senate, with a highly paid staff of Washington gun-slingers, and with no political experience whatsoever, but with a questionable record of personal behavior, and as the head of a company with multiple charges of dumping toxic wastes, a company known to be a major defense contractor [It's amazing how much you can "ask" in a 30-second question. Actually, AuCoin ran over the time limit but the moderator didn't stop him]; in view of all that, how can you have the audacity to want to put all these loggers and mill-workers in Oregon out of work, and destroy our economy?"

Huh?

This was hard ball! This was the major leagues. I was speechless for several seconds. How do you answer a "question" like that? ... in 60 seconds?! In my case, not very well. Totally flummoxed, I stumbled around trying to address all the lies and character attacks in his "question" and, when my time was up I simply and ignominiously stopped, mid-sentence. Score one for AuCoin.

Fortunately, the debate didn't end there. Regrouping, I fired one off at him for his campaign contributions, from the timber industry, from major defense contractors, from people far from here who mispronounced Oregon as "Ory-gone". Joe Wetzel was a participant in that first debate, too, and he fired off a round at AuCoin, too. "Go after the incumbent, the person most responsible for the corrupt mess back in Washington", was Wetzel's attitude, and my own.

But, again, League rules intervened. They said that we had to alternate the person to whom our questions were addressed. Here I had been waiting for two years to pummel a member of Congress on the national disgrace of election campaign bribes-known-as-contributions, and, instead, I had to direct a question to innocent Joe Wetzel.

Fortunately, AuCoin had a major vulnerability that provoked the average taxpayer. For some years prior to '92, many members of Congress used the congressional bank—from which they received their paychecks—as a kind of unlimited credit card, against which they could write checks for personal expenses without having the funds to cover them. AuCoin had written 80+ such checks, including one for more than $20,000 to remodel his kitchen in his Washington, D.C., home. The press got hold of the story and it became a national issue for some weeks. The congressional check-bouncing scandal was just beginning to unravel back in Washington, D.C., at that time, although we still didn't know the full extent of AuCoin's implication in the mess. And so my first question for Wetzel went something like this, "Joe, what happens if you bounce a check and how do you feel about members of Congress regularly kiting checks and asking us taxpayers to cover them while the insufficient funds are being made sufficient?"

AuCoin continued with his "questions" of me. It got so bad, in fact, that in the middle of one of his tirades, hissing and mild booing came from the audience. Our moderator, instead of admonishing AuCoin for his boorish behavior, admonished the audience. But the audience reaction worked: AuCoin toned it down afterwards.

And suddenly, just as quickly as it had started, it was over. We only got to ask a couple of questions of one another, and then the questions came from a press panel, assembled for the occasion. Their questions were at least fair, but they certainly weren't the kinds of questions *I* wanted to put to AuCoin. I knew his record in Congress, from our extensive research; they didn't. And so their questions were easily sidestepped, or even ignored, by someone who had been there before, and AuCoin had.

Somehow, when it was all over, I felt great. Partly, of course, simply because it was over. But people in the audience, including former Congressman Jim Weaver from Eugene, walked up and said that I had "creamed him" (it didn't seem so to me).

Debates in the League format are a joke. First, they're much too short, over all. The time for opening statements—a couple of minutes—isn't nearly enough. And in a hour, you might get to ask your opponent all of three questions. Second, the time for answering questions is much too short. Third, I would downplay, if not outright eliminate, the role of outside questioners, be they press or other "informed, unbiased" questioners.

Who better to ask the questions, and insist on honest answers, than the opponent? It's true that if only the principals ask and answer the questions it might get a little heated at times. So let it! If it got intense, people might actually come to the debates—not just as spectators, but to learn something. And the TV cameras might even cover the whole event if they knew there was going to be some *life* to them, so that people might watch on TV.

There were two TV cameras at our Grants Pass debate, one of them from Portland. But they didn't carry it live—why should they? No one would watch—and all they carried on the 11 o'clock news that evening was a few seconds of the "heat." My complaints to the League—state and national —about the format have fallen on deaf ears. It's a classic Catch 22: no substance, no viewers, no coverage.

The second debate was held in Portland, The Big Time. Mindful of AuCoin's tactics in Grants Pass, my debate-preparation crew *really* tore into me this time. The event was held in the giant ballroom of the Hilton hotel. There were close to 1000 people packed in, and *eight* TV cameras, including C-SPAN, which was covering it live. AuCoin's staff outdid us in packing the house; I would guess that 80% of the crowd were AuCoin supporters. It helped his confidence, and hurt mine. It was the same old unproductive format, but this time AuCoin was subdued. Sadly, Joe Wetzel wasn't invited to participate by the League of Women Voters.

In spite of all the debate preparation, I was scared to death. Major league dry-mouth. But I wasn't the only one. AuCoin and I shook hands before the debate began and, if my mouth was like the Sahara, his hand was like the Antarctic.

The debate itself was an anti-climax. No surprises: the timber issue, campaign finance reform, my inexperience, his Washington-insider status. The result: probably a nothing-nothing tie.

And the final debate, at Blue Mountain Community College in Pendleton, didn't settle anything either. Joe Wetzel was invited. No fireworks, little coverage.

# # #

Oregon is a peace-loving state. Partly, that's because no major defense contractors — like Boeing in nearby Seattle — chose to settle here, and there isn't one significant military base. Thus, we weren't exposed to years and years of propaganda from the entire military-industrial complex, about how a strong military prevents war. Mark Hatfield made his reputation in the U.S. Senate by being a strong anti-war advocate.

Les AuCoin sold himself as a peace advocate, too. At one time, he, Hatfield, and I all served on the board of the Oregon Peace Institute. But for every career politician, there's one thing much bigger than any issue, or any principle, and that's getting re-elected. And getting re-elected in the modern era means raising money to run your re-election campaign and, specifically, to pay for TV ads with which to bash your opponent. And AuCoin was as good at that as any of them, particularly with his seat on the Defense sub-committee of the House Appropriations Committee — the best money machine in Congress.

The young and likable researcher on our campaign staff, John Koehn, had come up with a stunning bit of AuCoin hypocrisy. Not surprisingly, AuCoin over the years had been a major recipient of campaign contributions from defense contractors—more than $100,000-worth in his House career. (How long would it take for me to raise $100,000 over the phone, I wondered, from good people who only wanted clean government?)

One particularly egregious example of peace-loving AuCoin kowtowing to the defense industry involved the B-2 bomber. That weapon system has caught a lot of flak over the years because of its enormous price-tag: just one of those puppies costs $2 billion, enough to build an entire university! In 1989, while the defense appropriations bill was working its way through the House, AuCoin took one of those junkets that Congresspersons are famous for, to each of the major B-2 contractors: Boeing in Seattle, Northrup and Hughes Aircraft in L.A., LTV in Dallas, etc, picking up $2000 in speaking honoraria at each stop, along with pledges of PAC support. It worked out to a tidy little $13,000 for him personally, on the side, for a week's work. And three weeks later, he voted to authorize another $3.9 billion for the B-2. (I was sitting on the Oregon Peace Institute board at the time, as was AuCoin, and the board was so incensed at AuCoin's double-dealing that it wrote him a strongly worded letter of protest. He then resigned from the board; but not from his defense-industry connections.)

Our campaign called a press conference, complete with a big graphic showing where AuCoin's defense money came from. It didn't seem to excite many people, except in the AuCoin camp. In fact, The Oregonian's headline over the article covering our press conference was "Lonsdale charge angers AuCoin camp", and more than half of "our" article was devoted to Rick Guregian, AuCoin's aggressive press secretary, calling us "damnable" liars, "dangerous ... desperate", and owing Les and the people of Oregon an apology! When you're caught in the act, the best defense is still a stiff offense.

While we were looking into AuCoin's massive PAC contributions, AuCoin was doing some snooping around, too. Word reached us that he had sent two staffers to my former high school in North Plainfield, New Jersey, from which I had graduated in 1949, to check on my school record and see what dirt they could find. Nothing seems to be out of bounds in this business.

# # #

Modern election campaigns go on for months, sometimes years, in our country. AuCoin declared in May of '91 for a November '92 general election. And I announced in September of '91. But, until the last few weeks, virtually nothing appears to be happening, to the outside world. The candidates are busily raising money, traveling the state, trying desperately for press coverage or, better yet, favorable TV coverage. But most people don't care about elections until they are only a few days away. And, unless you're an incumbent or you commit a felony, you just don't rate any TV coverage. They *sell* that stuff, they don't give it away!

But as the primary election time approached, in late April, early May, the big guns came out: the TV spots. Wetzel, of course, couldn't afford any, and so it was down to a two-person race for the Democratic nomination. According to the polls, 6 weeks out, it was a horse race, presumably because AuCoin was being hurt by the check-bouncing scandal.

All the work, 40,000 more miles on the odometer, the inevitable glitches, the verbal abuse, the house parties, the stress, debates, long days, fund-raising calls, our "Blueprint for Change", lawn signs, mailings, bumper stickers—all of that, and more, counted for very little. Where we stood on *issues*, sad to say, was secondary. What it comes down to in a contested election is *TV spots*. Who can afford the most, and how effective are they? ... effective, not in differentiating oneself from the opponent on an important issue, but effective at discrediting or raising doubts about your opponent. Oh, sure, you work in some positives about yourself, too, just so the voters will actually remember your name when they walk into the polling booth. But mostly the candidate's job is to find the opponent's weak spot, in focus groups if you can afford them (we couldn't, this time), and keep jabbing away at that spot until it bleeds.

From our point of view, AuCoin's weak spot was all those bounced checks. Now, on a scale from one to ten, where does congressional check-bouncing rank as a national issue? Maybe a "one." But as something to remind people of what was wrong back in Washington, D.C., and how out of touch with the real world many of those congresspeople were, it was a silver bullet. What I *really* wanted to say about AuCoin in our 30-second spots was something like this: Do you like having a $5 *trillion* national debt? — that's $20,000 for every man, woman, and child in America — Well, Les helped bring it to you. Do you like clearcuts in our national forests? Do you like spending $2 billion apiece for B-2 bombers we'll never use? Do you like feeling powerless about what goes on back in Washington, D.C.? Most important of all, by far: do you like how far we have sunk as a nation because of all those campaign contributions, the favors they buy and the corruption they exude? Well, if so, vote for the incumbent, and you'll get more of the same.

But what did we actually run, in the two negative TV spots that we could afford? Why, two check-bouncing spots. I had some misgivings about that. It certainly wasn't our main issue, except it illustrated the arrogance that goes with long-term incumbency.

AuCoin's spots were very effective, too. He resurrected the old Bhagwan stuff, projecting me as a big fan and accomplice of the guru. It had worked for Mark Hatfield, maybe it could still work. Apparently his focus groups told him it was still a hot issue. Because I had never held office and had never voted on *anything*, there wasn't much they could stick me with substantively — although I had certainly tried to make my positions ultra-clear with that comprehensive "Blueprint for Change."

AuCoin's other negative spot was clearly below the belt. When our negotiators had worked out the terms of our debate in Portland, one thing that both sides agreed to, in writing, was that no use would be made of any of the audio or video record of the debate. So what's in AuCoin's "attack" spot? Me, with my eyes shifting wildly about, left-to-right-to-left, with some eerie music in the background and with the announcer referring to me as a "shifty-eyed politician". I was shifty-eyed, all right, because they had taken the video of the debate and speeded it up to make it look like my eyes were darting around ... in direct conflict with our written agreement. But *me*, the shifty-eyed politician?! It stung but, I had to admit, it was effective, and in politics that's all that counts.

Our side got some important newspaper endorsements, including the Salem Statesman-Journal and the Medford Mail Tribune. Not The Oregonian, of course. I was too much the outsider, too much the tree-hugger, too uncontrollable for them. Besides, we all knew that The Oregonian would endorse Packwood in the general election in November.

Toward crunch time, Bob Packwood, who had an uncontested Republican primary, started running anti-AuCoin ads on the radio. That was a shocker to us—perhaps even unprecedented. All we could figure was that Packwood felt that I would be the easier opponent to defeat in the fall —easier, because I couldn't raise the kind of money that AuCoin could.

# # #

On Sunday, just two days before the May 19, 1992 primary, we were dealt a double blow by The Oregonian. On the front page, they carried the results of the latest poll that they had commissioned. It had us way behind AuCoin, 48-33%. We found that result preposterous, because all of the other polls we had seen about that time had the race neck and neck. Still, this was from the newspaper of record in Oregon, so the story had weight. It also had the obvious potential of depressing our vote; why should our strongest supporters go to the polls or carry our banners on election day if we were clearly going to lose?

Things got even worse on the editorial page that day. The Oregonian, like many newspapers, endorses candidates several weeks out from the election and then reminds their readers once or twice more, along the way, about who they were endorsing and why. The Sunday paper continued in that tradition. But instead of singing AuCoin's praises, they threw in this little keeper about me, right near the top of their long editorial: "Harry Lonsdale has run a low and dishonest campaign against AuCoin." It hurt. I'm still at a loss to explain it. I return to that little smear in the Press chapter, below.

# # #

Election day, May 19, finally arrived, after the usual counting of the days, hours, minutes. Here's a hint as to the outcome: AuCoin raised and spent $1.5 million on the campaign, much of it from PACs, more than half of his money from out-of-state. Like us, he spent most of it on TV ads. We raised and spent $500,000, a little over half of it my own money, none of it from PACs again, almost all of it from within Oregon.

When the polls closed at 8 p.m. and the TV cameras showed up at our campaign headquarters for the rare open-mike opportunity, we were ahead by some 5000 votes statewide, but with a huge number of Portland metro votes still to be counted. All through that long night, our lead dwindled. By the time I went to bed at 1 a.m. our lead was down to 1000 votes, and when I got up the next morning, we were behind by 200 votes. And it fluctuated around a bit all day, settling in on a "final" lead for AuCoin of 328 votes—out of more than 360,000 votes cast. (What ever happened to his 48-33% lead in the poll just two days before? we wondered.)

Oregon election law provides for an automatic recount in any election decided by less than 0.2%. In our case, the difference was actually less than 0.1%—less than 1 voter per precinct!

Recounts take time, of course—two weeks, in our case. In the meantime there was nothing to do but wait, relax, go back home to Bend —and go fishing, which I did. But the recount didn't change the result. When it was all said and done, we had lost by 330 votes.

We had actually won in 27 of Oregon's 36 counties. AuCoin carried essentially the counties he had represented in Congress for 18 years. The final Oregonian poll hurt us some—several people called or wrote to tell me that they didn't even bother to vote because it appeared certain that we had lost—and The Oregonian's editorial surely didn't help us, either. But, in the end, it was Joe Wetzel who probably decided the outcome. Wetzel garnered 25,000 votes, most of which were presumably anti-incumbent votes and therefore "my" votes. Mitzi Scott sensed, near the end, that Wetzel's presence in the race could be decisive, and she strongly encouraged me to call him and try to get him to step aside. I wouldn't. First, I felt that anyone has a right to run and if they're willing to take the heat, more power to them. On the practical side, I didn't think Wetzel could be dissuaded. Mitzi *did* call him, in the end, against my wishes, but to no avail.

A short post-script: AuCoin lost the general election in November to Packwood, 52-48%, who proved in their debates to be a superior debater—"masterful" might be more accurate. He didn't hit AuCoin with the same fund-raising stuff I had, since he, Packwood, was guilty—guiltier, in fact —of pursuing the same sleazy special-interest money that AuCoin went after.

In his concession press conference, when asked what he would do next, after a near lifetime in politics, AuCoin allowed that he didn't know yet, but whatever it was, he'd never become a lobbyist. But within a matter of weeks, he was not only hired by one of the major inside-the-beltway lobbying firms, he was lobbying for the timber industry!

Harry Lonsdale

The Packwood story is now well known. All through 1992 rumors were swirling around Oregon about Packwood's multi-year sexual harassment of women. But the story never made the press until, once again, it was broken by The Washington Post, just days *after* the November election. And when it couldn't affect the election, even The Oregonian reported on it and then slammed him unmercifully in its editorials. It took two years, a flock of Jay Leno jokes on the late-night tube, signed affidavits from a dozen or more of the women he had harassed — some of whom had made their charges years earlier, only to be ignored by the "ever-vigilant" press — but Packwood finally resigned in disgrace, one of a handful of U.S. Senators to do so in the entire history of the country. And now, he, too, is a high powered lobbyist back in Washington, D.C.

# # #

It seems so trivial, and yet I'll remember it forever. When it was over, and we had lost the primary, two of our workaholic staffers, John Koehn and Wyatt Closs, presented me with a baseball cap. It was one of the old Brooklyn Dodger caps. They knew I was a life-long Dodger fan. And under the brim they had written with a bold felt pen, "You can't play the game unless you step up to the plate." I've still got that cap.

CHAPTER 4.

...TRY, TRY AGAIN

Fast-forward to 1995.

The following year would be a Senate election year in Oregon again: the Hatfield seat was up. And, with stories flying in the media about Bob Packwood's sexual harassment of women over a multi-year period, it was conceivable that he could be impeached, or, more likely, forced to resign.

Hatfield had his own set of scandals by this time. Not long after the 1990 election, The Washington Post broke the story of his accepting some expensive gifts from the president of the University of South Carolina while his son was attending the university on scholarship and while the senator was voting for a $15 million appropriation for a new engineering building there. And there were similar stories about his daughter, a scholarship student at Oregon Health Sciences University, and Hatfield's delivery of massive pork, in the form of construction funds, to the university. Months after The Washington Post broke the story it finally appeared in The Oregonian. But, like the charges of impropriety when Hatfield's wife received $60,000 for redecorating Basil Tsakos' Washington, D.C., apartment while the senator was trying to grease the way in the Senate for Tsakos' multi-billion-dollar trans-African oil pipeline, Hatfield successfully dodged those bullets. The South Carolina furor ended with the Senate voting to rebuke Hatfield, a relatively mild form of censure.

For some months, I weighed the possibility of taking on Hatfield again. I had done well against him the first time, and it seemed that no one else would challenge him: certainly no viable Republican, and even Oregon's most visible Democrats, like Congressman Peter DeFazio, were saying publicly that Hatfield was too valuable to Oregon to lose.

As usual there was the big downside to running, for me: the inevitable beating I would take from the press, my hatred of fund raising, the fear of losing and the rejection and depression that went with it, and, even if I won, the concerns about serving day-to-day in a chamber with the likes of Orrin Hatch, Alan Simpson, and Arlen Specter, three "distinguished gentlemen" who had so unfairly and unmercifully torn apart Anita Hill during the confirmation hearings for Supreme Court Justice Clarence Thomas.

After two tough Senate losses, I was feeling upbeat in '95. Most importantly, I had fallen in love with and married a wonderful woman, and thus had someone to share all those hopes and fears with. And in 1992, Oregonians had voted overwhelmingly, by initiative, in favor of term limits for in-state elected officials: 70% of us had voted in favor. If ever there was a poster-boy for term limits, it was 5-term Senator Mark Hatfield.

I was also feeling buoyed up by the Perot phenomenon still lingering from '92. While I doubted that I would like Perot-the-Man, I certainly was enamored of Perot-the-Message. His "take back your country" slogan and his talk of an electronic town hall echoed some of my own thoughts, as they did for millions of Americans. Of course, Perot had the luxury—an *earned* luxury, to be sure—of being able to get his message out with his own money. How many Americans are ever in that position? And, of those few that are, only a handful ever take advantage of it.

After my usual waffling, I decided to seriously test the waters. I would travel the entire state, all 36 counties, one more time, with my pitch to see if the support was there. Fortunately, I had a wide cadre of friends built up from the '90 and '92 campaigns spread out across the state, and I asked them for help with the local arrangements. I printed up volunteer cards and passed them out at every meeting, asking people to commit to either contributing money or contributing time to the campaign effort. And I toted around sign-up sheets wherever I went. I started the exploratory campaign very early—in February 1995—a full 21 months before the November '96 general election and 15 months before the May primary. I've never been much of a sprinter and I felt that, given enough of a head start, I could make it this time. There were a lot of friendships to re-establish, and a lot of money to raise—but first I had to decide if the race was worth making.

I also decided at the very beginning that I wasn't going to finance my own campaign again. I had already spent most of my life's savings in '90 and '92 and I felt that if Oregonians wanted me for their senator, a few thousand of them would have to cough up $50 or $100 each to elect me. This would be a grassroots campaign, which was what I had wanted to do earlier but lacked the courage and the friends to pull it off. I committed a maximum of $25,000 of my own money, if I decided to run, as seed money, to get the campaign off the ground. I would do no polling, and hire no out-of-state campaign strategists. If I hadn't learned all that those pros had to teach me the first two times, I was a poor student. I also decided to neither solicit nor accept any out-of-state money. And, of course, I wasn't accepting any PAC money.

It was essential to my candidacy that my supporters get involved, and not just with a check. A documentary movie was made of the '92 Clinton presidential campaign, starring James Carville and George Stephanopoulos. It's called "The War Room". In the movie, after Clinton has pulled off the unlikely victory, Carville calls the troops together in the war room for a victory rally and thank-you speech. His words were stirring. He knew better than anyone just how hard those young people in the room had worked. And he said something like, "You know, there's something that we just don't honor enough in this country, and that is *work*! You have honored this campaign by giving of yourself, by giving your *work*." It was that kind of spirit I was hoping I could inject into the '96 campaign. My self-doubts had vanished. I knew that running again was the right thing to do and, *if we could raise the money and turn out the workers*, we could win this time.

Good things started happening almost immediately after we started the exploratory campaign. Dana Hanson Nehl, my trusted secretary and good right arm for several years, signed on, as did three other great volunteers: Judy Hanlon, Nancy Ridings, and Jo Zucker, all from Bend. Several dozen others offered to help stuff envelopes. My wife, Bryn Hazell, while mindful of what my two prior unsuccessful runs had cost me, was fully supportive.

And then it was back on the road: an opening event in Bend, where I honed my stump speech, and then on to Ashland (what better place to start a Democratic campaign?), Jacksonville, Medford, Gold Beach, Brookings, Port Orford, Coos Bay, North Bend, Grants Pass, Florence, Waldport, Newport, Corvallis, Eugene, Albany, Monmouth, Salem, Tillamook, Lincoln City, Cannon Beach, McMinnville, Wilsonville, Portland (for a full week), St. Helens, Astoria, Lake Oswego, Hood River, The Dalles, Condon, Hermiston, Pendleton, Baker City, La Grande, Enterprise, John Day, Ontario, Burns, Klamath Falls, Lakeview, Madras, and Prineville, with a few stops back home in Bend along the way to do my laundry. If you want to get to know the people and the geography of your state, run for statewide office!

In the end, I had visited all 36 counties, had lined up chairpersons that we felt we could count on in each county, and had collected hundreds of volunteer cards, with pledges of thousands of hours of work and tens of thousands of dollars in contributions. And it was still only June 1995! I announced my candidacy on June 30, in Portland, in some friends' offices. The TV cameras showed up. It was an auspicious start. No one else was in the race at this early juncture, not even Mark Hatfield, who hadn't yet decided whether he would run again.

# # #

But the euphoria didn't last long. The head of the Oregon Democratic Party that year was an irascible woman named Jana Doerr. She was quoted in the paper as saying that I was unelectable. Unelectable?! Ask Mark Hatfield or Les AuCoin if I was unelectable. And then Bob Stoll, a former supporter and the vice-chair of the state party, was in the paper saying that he sure hoped that "someone besides Lonsdale would run." With friends like these ...! Somehow he didn't feel that same way back in '92 when Les AuCoin was the first Democrat to announce. Then, one Democratic candidate seemed to be plenty for Bob Stoll; he had asked me not to run against AuCoin.

I came awfully close, at that point, to doing something that I had been tempted to do since 1990: run as an Independent. There were several good reasons. First, what had the Democratic Party of Oregon ever done for me? Second, Independents don't have to run in the primary, thereby saving a lot of money and wear-and-tear; they go directly to the general election in the fall. Third, I was an Independent at heart, partly because the Democratic Party was just as corrupt as the Republican party, and partly because the Democratic Party—the "New Democrats", as Clinton called them—had abandoned most of the Party principles set out by Jefferson, Jackson, FDR, Truman, Kennedy, and Johnson. In the end, reason prevailed: Independents don't win!

And then the reality of campaigning set in: the endless hours and miles of driving; the frustration of fund-raising calls, most of which were unsuccessful that early in the campaign; the usual cast of hecklers and arguers in every audience, people who wanted me to agree with them on every issue, including *their* hot-button issue; and, most importantly, the people who pledged to help in one way or another, and didn't. Nothing is as depressing as friends who let you down.

My one-man campaign ground along that way—press "hits", fund-raising calls, stump speeches, and miles and miles of driving—through the summer and fall of '95. We hired a campaign manager, a nice young man named Gordon Heady, as our only paid staff member. I came to like Gordy, even though he knew even less about campaigning than I did. But he had some positive qualities, too: he was bright, ambitious, an Oregonian by birth, an ardent supporter, and he was *affordable*. In our low-budget campaign, we couldn't afford any of those $5,000 - $10,000 per month East Coast pros.

And then Bob Packwood abruptly resigned. Almost immediately, Democratic Congressman Ron Wyden, who had been hoarding his leftover campaign cash for just such an opportunity, jumped into the race to fill the Packwood vacancy. So did Democratic Congressman Peter DeFazio, from Eugene. And so did up-and-coming Republican State Senator Gordon Smith, who was already Senate president at the tender age of 42.

I thought about it briefly, of course, but decided against. True, it was an open U.S. Senate seat, and those don't come along very often. But Wyden already had close to a million dollars in the till, and Gordon Smith was worth $20 million personally and was claiming that he would spend "whatever it took". At that point, we had $10,000 in our campaign account, and there was no way we could raise the million it would take to be competitive in the few weeks left before the election. We stayed out. My good friend and fellow tree-hugger, Michael Donnelly of Salem, filed for the seat. He had no money and thus not a prayer of winning. But he came up with a catchy campaign slogan. Voting for DeFazio or Wyden, he said, was "voting for the evil of two lessers." It's one thing to have a great message; it's something else entirely to have the ability (read "money") to deliver your message to the voters. Donnelly didn't.

Wyden narrowly beat DeFazio in the Democratic primary, massively outspending him. Smith won the Republican primary unopposed. And Wyden beat Smith in the general election to become Oregon's first Democratic Senator in almost 30 years. Smith and Wyden, between them, spent well over $5 million on the race.

And then, in late November 1995, Mark Hatfield announced he wouldn't run for re-election. *Two* Senate vacancies in one year! And, almost instantaneously, I went from being the lone Democrat seeking the office to one of five! Jerry Rust, a long-term Lane County commissioner and a fellow tree-hugger, jumped in. (No money.) Bill Dwyer, a two-term State Senator from Springfield and an outspoken supporter of timber workers, jumped in. (No money.) Anna Nevenich, a total unknown and part-time nurse, jumped in. (No money.) And Tom Bruggere, a "Hatfield Democrat" who refused to support me in 1990 or 1992, a co-founder of Mentor Graphics, one of Oregon's most successful high tech firms, jumped in. Unlike the others, he had personal wealth of $20 million, he said, and he was prepared to spend whatever it took. And Gordon Smith announced on the Republican side, his second Senate race in just a matter of months.

I wondered, of course, if my statewide name identification and my corps of volunteers would be enough to hold off Bruggere's money. Name-I.D., after all, can be bought, just as I had bought mine in 1990. And my name-I.D. was already aging. I had last run in 1992, and didn't even make it to the general election. And so a lot of people had forgotten me, while other supporters had died or moved out-of-state. Name-I.D. has to be frequently nourished. People who sell lists for a living advertise the *age* of their list, along with the demographic data.

I needn't have bothered to worry. When Bruggere announced that he would be spending *real* money on the race, I was a goner, even though I didn't know it at the time. I continued to plow ahead, however, under the delusion that my previous experience and my corps of volunteers would carry me through. Meanwhile, Nebraska Senator Bob Kerrey, like Bruggere a Vietnam War veteran and also head of the Democratic Senatorial Campaign Committee, virtually declared, in *Time* Magazine and elsewhere, that Bruggere was the Party's choice. He had money, making him competitive with Gordon Smith, the Republican.

Then the endorsements started to roll in—solidly for Bruggere. Organizational endorsements come after the candidate has passed through a screening process, which usually includes a thorough questionnaire. I'm sure that I scored 100% on most of those questionnaires, but Bruggere got the endorsements: from NARAL, even from the Oregon League of Conservation Voters, and (shame on them) the Oregon Natural Resources Council. I had spent years championing the forests, and Tom Bruggere wasn't even an environmentalist. "Hey, Harry, he's not as good as you are on the forests but he's acceptable on the other environmental issues ... and he's better than Smith ... and he has money!" (Within days of that ONRC treachery, five people wrote or phoned me to tell me they were taking ONRC out of their will. Within six months, I had taken them out of my will, too. Bruggere wasn't even opposed to clearcuts.)

We had some debates, the five of us Democrats, although they were perfunctory at best. Except for Bill Dwyer attacking Bruggere for trying to steal the election with his money, the debates were friendly, and dull. On most issues we actually agreed, although we emphasized different things.

Jerry Rust gained my respect, early on. He had been busted for drugs several years earlier, and rather than try to hide the fact he put out a preemptive press release announcing it. Had he not done so, no one would probably ever have been the wiser.

Our campaign had our usual issues, updated, of course, but we couldn't afford to advertise them widely. We published an extensive set of issue positions in a mailing that went to 100,000 Oregonians. But that still meant that more than three million Oregonians never saw them.

Bob Young, a reporter for Willamette Week, a Portland alternative newspaper, asked all five of us Democratic candidates to prepare our version of a balanced federal budget. He said he'd print the results in his newspaper. I dug into that project with gusto. *(Anything* but make those fund-raising calls!) And it was great fun, like being "King for a Day". On paper, at least, I could tax and spend, cut and supplement federal expenditures any way I wanted to. He who controls the purse strings controls the country. Everyone should try their hand at preparing their version of the national budget, whether balanced or not.

Here's what my balanced budget looked like, in broad-brush:

> Raise income taxes on large corporations.
> Raise the federal tax on gasoline.
> Raise tobacco and alcohol taxes.
> Raise import duties on U.S. companies manufacturing overseas.
> Increase the inheritance tax on the wealthy.
> End corporate welfare.
> Cut capital-gains tax rates for job-creation only, but raise income
>   taxes on the wealthy.
> Cut military spending sharply.

> Apply "means-testing" to seniors on Social Security.
> Increase money for student college loans, and for Americorps.
> Increase funding for civilian research and development.
> Increase funding for international birth control.
> Reduce farm subsidies.
> Spend money on low-income housing.
> Increase funding for mass transit.
> Restore the national forests and salmon runs.
> ...And more.

Even with all the increased expenditures, I came up with a $2 billion surplus in the year 2000 by raising taxes on those that could afford them, cutting the military, and ending corporate welfare. (Clinton's budgets for his remaining years in office actually showed a surplus, but that was because of a booming economy, not any major reorientation of national priorities.)

I confess that the basis for my thinking was Paul Hawken's notion, espoused in his book, "The Ecology of Commerce". Hawken says this: "If you want to change things, save the environment, reduce consumerism, or whatever, then do it with *taxes*. Tax those things heavily that you *don't* want, and provide tax incentives, even rebates, for those things you *do* want." It sounds simple. It might even work. Will we ever try?

I was the only one of the five Democratic candidates to provide a detailed response to Bob Young's request and Willamette Week never published any of our responses. The Oregonian gave us a nice write-up on it, however.

# # #

In the end, it was no contest. Bruggere had a well-oiled, professional campaign staff on board, and they started the public part of the campaign with mailings of full-color, glossy brochures to every registered Democrat in the state. Then came his TV blitz. All positive, all well done, all run multiple times statewide. We put together two TV spots, one of which was the best one we ever did. It talked about what I wanted for our country — no attack ads from me this time! It was designed and produced by my wife, Bryn, and a very creative friend, Michael Marx. But we only had the money to run it a few times around the state. None of the other Democrats in the primary had any money to run *any* statewide TV ads.

Over the last few weeks prior to the May 19, 1996 primary, the result was never in doubt. The only question remaining was "how much would Bruggere win by?"

A lot. The final statewide results were Bruggere 50%, Lonsdale 25%, Rust 10%, Dwyer 10%, and Nevenich 5%. It was a blowout. We were outspent by Bruggere 10 to 1 — $1.3 million to $130,000. The other Democrats were outspent by even greater ratios.

In the general election in the fall, Gordon Smith beat Tom Bruggere 52-48% in a largely negative campaign. Between them, Smith and Bruggere spent more than $6 million on the race, much of it their own money. They both accepted copious PAC money.

# # #

If you've never run for elected office and lost, there's probably no way you can understand what it feels like. I've often felt, ever since that fateful November 6, 1990, that we losers should form a club, "The Losers Club", where we get together once a year over a couple of beers, tell our tales, and have a good cry.

All of us have lost, at one thing or another. I played junior varsity basketball in high school. We lost at least as many games as we won. Sure it hurt — for about an hour. But not many of my fellow students showed up for the J.V. basketball games, so there was little embarrassment in losing. And, besides, there was always a nice hot shower after the game, and a good night's sleep, and, heck, there was next week's game against Dunellen. We could *always* beat Dunellen.

It's not that way when you lose a hard-fought statewide election. First, because it's *very* public. Every newspaper, radio station, and TV station in the state is pouring out the news, the gory details of how many counties your opponent won (and you lost), his big victory party at the Hilton — with half of the Democratic big-wigs in the state there, licking his boots and buying him champagne. Meanwhile, you're sitting in the nearly empty campaign headquarters with a few remaining diehards, trying to drink a warm beer while you hold back the tears. (Actually, our '96 campaign had a bittersweet election night. We had a big party at a Portland restaurant. Even though Bruggere was obviously the winner early on, our supporters cheered and cheered for what we'd all attempted, and we dedicated ourselves to "keep on fighting the good fight." We danced the night away.)

Second, there's all the *work*—all those volunteers stuffing all those envelopes; all the hundreds of hours behind the wheel of the car, visiting every city, town, and hamlet in Oregon; all the speech prep, the fund-raising events, the fear, frustration, anger, fatigue. And the staff, bless their hearts; they worked harder than I did, and came up with nothing but some puny paychecks and maybe a few new friends.

Third, there's heartbreak—yours and your supporters'. We really did believe in our issues, and we really wanted a better America.

And, finally, there *is* no game next week against Dunellen. It's *over*. Few things in life are as final or as abrupt as an election result. Some people you don't even know, scattered across the state, count a million-plus pieces of paper, someone announces the result and, bamm-o, you're unemployed. Hey, what do I *do* tomorrow? No schedule? No road trips? No press conference? No *fund-raising* calls?!

A story went around about Republican Norma Paulus' loss to Neil Goldschmidt in the 1986 Oregon governor's race. I've always admired Norma for the same reasons that I admired Wayne Morse and Barry Goldwater: what you saw was what you got: no B.S. I wish that I had voted for her in '86. But I didn't, we didn't, and she lost. It was said that she went into a nosedive after the loss. Even a six-month vacation in Mexico, far from any Oregonians, didn't rehabilitate her. It was two years before she entered the ring again. She became Oregon's Superintendent of Public Instruction, a statewide, elected office.

After three losing Senate campaigns, I knew how she felt.

CHAPTER 5.

FUND RAISING

The summer after the '96 primary was over, but before the general election in November, I'd walk down the streets of Bend or Portland or Eugene, and people would hail me and ask, "Hey, Harry, are you running for the Senate this year? I'll vote for you again." They didn't even know that I'd lost the primary. With no money for TV ads, there's simply no candidacy. And that's what I want to return to here: the overwhelming importance of money in American electoral politics today, and how it is raised.

Records from the Federal Election Commission show that the Hatfield campaign raised a million dollars in October 1990, when the polls showed our race almost dead even, and that almost every penny of that money was raised from PACs and that few of those PACs represented Oregonians. Most of the money was used, with devastating effect on me, to run negative TV ads.

I contend that if Mark Hatfield had died in the summer of 1990, but that it hadn't been reported in the press, and that if he had prepared some radio and TV spots before he died that were then aired during the fall campaign, *he would still have won*! He didn't need to shake one hand, give one stump speech, drive one mile, he didn't have to debate, he didn't even have to show up. But he had to have that last million dollars to run those TV ads.

A modern election campaign is something like a shooting war. But instead of shooting bullets at each other, the candidates shoot television ads. Unlike real bullets, those TV ads, in a relatively small population state like Oregon, cost a minimum of *$100,000* a piece, even in 1990, and the price keeps escalating. (In California, with 10 times Oregon's population, a TV "bullet" costs several million dollars.) So, what is a TV "bullet"? It is a single, 30-second message on all of the state's TV stations, saying something favorable about oneself or something unfavorable about one's opponent, repeated sufficiently frequently that the average adult TV viewer will see it enough times to remember it, regardless of the types of TV shows he or she watches regularly. Back in 1990, during our

Hatfield campaign, that meant running the ad several times a day on each of the then-three major network channels (ABC, CBS, and NBC) in each television market. Here in the 21st Century, with the advent of more and more cable TV channels, it becomes even harder and more expensive to reach TV viewers. Cable TV now reaches the vast majority of American homes, meaning that the audience is highly fragmented.

In Oregon, we're talking about perhaps $300,000 in the year 2000 to produce and deliver that single message via TV to the average voter. That's one "bullet". And the war, all other things being equal, is predictably won by the campaign with the most bullets. There are exceptions, of course, as when one of the candidates commits some major boo-boo during or prior to the campaign. And all other things are *not* equal, the incumbent having great advantages over the challenger in name I.D. and in many other ways, as we've already noted. But, to a first approximation, this war is decided by how many bullets you can afford.

Let's say you can afford four—that's $1,200,000, minimum, for TV ads in a state like Oregon. And let's say your opponent can afford six bullets. Let's say that you fire your four bullets, one a week for the last four weeks of the campaign. And let's say that your opponent duplicates your efforts for the first two weeks of the TV war, but then has four bullets left (to your two) for the final two weeks of the campaign. Unless your opponent is an idiot, or is overendowed with principle, he or she will use two or three of the last four bullets to make some attack against you. It needn't be true; it could even be defamatory. (If the attack ads are too raunchy, of course, the TV stations can refuse to run them; they could get sued. But that very rarely happens.) So, here you sit, with a pack of lies or distortions being spread about you into virtually every home in the state, and you're not able to respond with your defense, let alone carry out an assault on your opponent. If you use your last two bullets to answer his two attacks, you're out of ammo. And he isn't yet. Game over.

I've oversimplified things, of course. Even today, no election campaign is totally dependent on TV ads, although we are now distressingly close to that state. There are other factors, to be sure: the candidates' positions on issues, their prior track records, radio and newspaper ads, direct mail ads, press reports, endorsements, how many thousands of handshakes you make, even lawn signs, bumper stickers, and lapel buttons. But TV is "where it's at." I predict that one of these days, in the not-too-distant future, some smart candidate will win a race spending every advertising dime on TV ads. And election campaigns will never be the same again.

The scenario I've just presented, admittedly simplistic, pretty much describes what happened in our 1990 Senate campaign. The Hatfield camp had more bullets left in the final couple of weeks than we did, they fired those bullets with focus-group-driven precision, and they won. His incumbency helped, specifically in his being able to raise lots of money, but my being a fresh face helped me, too. The anti-incumbent mood was pervasive, even back then. The bottom line: count the money and, more often than not, you can anoint the winner.

And so, when the naive would-be candidate walks optimistically through the doors of the Democratic or Republican House or Senate campaign committee offices back in Washington, D.C., he or she is going to be shocked to hear the first question out of the mouths of the pros: "How much money can you raise? How much can your opponent raise? O.K., we can pretty well guess who wins." Forget where the two of you stand on the issues, forget why you're even running. How much money can you raise?

# # #

The first thing to know about campaign fund raising is that it's the ugliest, most degrading job in the world. I have dug ditches, shoveled tons of chicken manure, slopped hogs, pulled the guts out of many a chicken and turkey, gone door-to-door in sales campaigns, but nothing compares with personal political fund raising for the sheer indignity, humiliation, and degradation of it.

When you make fund-raising telephone calls for United Way or for Planned Parenthood—and I've done a bit of that, too—and people tell you "no", somehow it's not a personal rejection. O.K., so they don't believe in United Way, or they "already gave," or they're "maxed out" on their charitable giving for the year; there's no personal rejection when they say "no," and there are a hundred different ways of saying "no" without once uttering the word, I've discovered.

Even the Mormon missionaries who come to my door, or the Seventh Day Adventists with their Watchtower magazine—and, mind you, those jobs take a lot of guts, and I have a lot of sympathy for them; I've learned to try to let them down easy with words like "it's nothing personal, but..." — even when you say "no" to them, it's not a *personal* rejection.

But when it's *you* on the phone, asking for money for *your* election campaign, and they say "no", however they choose to say it, it hurts. Ten "nos" in a row and you're ready to quit for the day, even though it's only 9:30 a.m.

But I've gotten ahead of myself. First, of course, you have to *get* the prospect on the phone. It's not easy. Just who *are* the prospects? For the novice candidate, it's a combination of everybody you ever knew plus every list of prospective contributors that you can get your hands on. In my case, having lived and made friends in five states and having been in business for 15 years, I had an extensive Christmas card list, and an even more extensive business card file—probably approaching a thousand names. Virtually every one of those people got a fund-raising letter from me—many with personalized notes —followed up with a phone call. Every salesperson who ever called on Bend Research, the owners of the travel agency we used, the supplier of our chemicals, our garbage service, building contractor, architect, lawyer, accountant, my personal physician, optometrist—no one was immune. Even selected members of our staff got hit. (It's unfair, I know, but this was *war*.)

Then there are lists: environmentalists, pro-choice women's groups, known Democratic contributors all across the country, pro-Israel groups, any one with whom I might have some kind of affinity.

First, we'd send the letter, carefully crafted to that particular group. There are people who make a living designing those letters, for a price. I found those professionally crafted letters too flowery, too filled with unkeepable promises, too boastful; and so I wrote my own.

And then comes the phone call. The first bit of fun is in attempting to get the prospect on the phone. For every prospect, someone on the staff had prepared a call sheet for me: name, nickname, if any; spouse's name, if known; address and phone (work and home); title/position/profession; something personal about them, if known: ("loves baseball, Cubs fan"); previous contributions to Democratic candidates, if known; and then the all-important "request level": was this a potential $1000 contributor (the maximum allowed by federal election law), or a $250 contributor? It's a very handy bit of information to know, when you reach the closure part of the conversation. Don't ask for $250 if the person can give $1000. We rarely knew this level, and so I was usually flying blind.

But first we have to get the prospect on the *phone*, and in many cases, that involved a duel with the personal secretary: the candidate's enemy-number-one. Anyone who has risen to the level of having a personal secretary has trained her or him to *keep people like me away*, and they're very good at it. After several months of dueling with the best of them—and all too frequently losing—I came to think of them as the alligators in the moat.

Here's a sample dialogue with the alligator:

Me: "Hello (in a cheery voice, brimming with optimism), is John Jones in, please?"

Now, there are a variety of opening lines from me: "Hello, I'm calling for John Jones." Or "This is Harry Lonsdale calling for John Jones." Or, if unsure that I've called the right number, "I'm trying to reach John Jones."

For every move on my part, there's a countermove by the secretary. Let's assume that the secretary is a woman and the prospect is a man. Remember, her job is to keep me away from her boss!

If I haven't already identified myself, it could go like this:

She: "May I tell him who's calling, please?"

It seems like progress. He appears to be in, at least.
"Harry Lonsdale".
One time out of ten, you get lucky and she puts you through directly. More typically ...
"And may I tell him what this call is about?"
Uh oh, trouble.
"I'm running for the U.S. Senate, and I wanted to discuss my campaign with John."
Two cheats, there. I don't necessarily know "John." And I don't want to "discuss my campaign with him." I want to ask him for *money*. But she knows that anyway.

Decision point. I'm holding my breath. Am I going to get to talk with Mr. Jones, or aren't I? My fate is in her hands. Several possible outcomes here.

"I'm sorry, Mr. Jones is unavailable. (Pretty tough to get around that defense.) Or, "He's in a conference." Or, "He's on another line." Sometimes followed with, "Can I take your number and have him call you back?" Sometimes it's, "I'm sorry but Mr. Jones is out of the office today", which is totally at odds with her opening line of, "Can I tell him who's calling?"

Now, nine times out of ten, I suspect, he *is* available even when the secretary says he isn't, but she knows he's not going to want to talk with me. How to respond? If he's "on another line", it's easy: "I'd be glad to hold". But, more typically ...

"I really would like to talk with him, and it's probably best if I call him again rather than ask him to try to reach me. When would be a good time for me to call again?

This really should work. It should be "check" or "checkmate". But no...

"I don't have his calendar in front of me." Or, "I don't keep his schedule. Give me your number and I'll ask him to call you." Or, "I'll have him call you".. Or "I'll tell him you called." (No commitment there.)

Next call sheet.

Eventually, of course, you do usually get to speak with the prospect. So you'd better be prepared with your pitch. In the beginning, I scripted it, that is, I wrote it out, tried to commit it to memory, or, when that failed, just read the opening line from my notes. But, after a few dozen calls, it just flowed. If it was a totally cold call, that is, if I knew absolutely nothing about the prospect or why he or she might be inclined to part with $500 to this unknown candidate, I had a generic pitch, which went like this:

"Hello, I'm Harry Lonsdale, and I'm running for the U.S. Senate. Do you have a few minutes to talk now, or should I call back later? [Now is O.K.] Fine. Well, as you may know, I'm a scientist by training, and I started a successful high tech business in Bend some years back called Bend Research. We develop pollution-control equipment and other environmentally beneficial products. I'm running as a Democrat, and my key issues are protecting the Oregon environment and trying to restore some ethics to our government. Actually, I sent you a letter a couple of weeks ago, with some information. Did you have a chance to look at it? [Yes. Thanks. Interesting.] (Probably glanced at it and tossed it, as I normally do.) Well then, tell me, what's on your mind? Are you pleased with what's going on back in Congress? If not, what are your issues, and how can we work together to bring about some changes? (Then follows 1, or 5, or 10 minutes of dialogue, on a huge variety of issues, some of which I'm not familiar with. But when we've found some areas of agreement and it's time for closure...) "Say, John, this is going to be an expensive race. If I'm going to win, I'll have to buy TV ads, and they're horribly expensive. I'm going to spend a good deal of my own money to win this Senate seat, but I'm asking like-minded people to help with a financial contribution." (Deep breath) "Would you be in a position to make a $500 contribution at this time?" (Tension. Listening carefully.) [Rarely ... "Yes".] "Oh, that's great! Look, we'll send you an envelope with our return address. I'm really grateful, John." (If John has seemed supportive but declines my opening gambit.) "Well, if not, could you do $250?" (If still wavering) "$100?" (If another form of "no", maybe with just a *hint* of encouragement...) Well, could I try you again later? It's a long way till November, and I'd really like your help at some point. Is there some other way that you'd be willing to help; maybe host a coffee in your home?..."

Next call.
And so it went, fifty times a day, six days a week.

# # #

My initial fund-raising calls were ineffective. I didn't close the deal at the end of the call, I didn't ask for a specific amount, I didn't stress the urgency, and I didn't *beg*! So, Karen Olick, my '90 campaign manager, called back to Washington, D.C., and brought out an expert to coach me. I'll never forget him: Scott Gale, a real pro. (Gale helped Ron Wyden win a Senate seat in 1996.) Gale sat with me for two days, critiquing, listening to every nuance and advising me. I got better. But I didn't like myself as much.

Gale told me that there are three reasons why people give money to candidates:

1. Friendships, family, or some kind of bond. The trouble with calling those people is that you test the relationship every time. The fear of rejection is even greater than usual.

2. Issues and Access. People want to see you in office because you agree with them on their key issue. So, you've got to know what their key issue *is* – and since you rarely do, in advance, you've got to probe around for it. When you've found it, you make note of it, for a later call. Something that always worried me was this: if they're sending me money because of an issue, will they ever attempt to collect, that is, will they use their paid-for access to my Senate office to try to get me to vote their way on a bill that I disagree with on principle, or modify a bill to suit them or suppress a bill unfavorable to them? I never won a Senate seat, so it never happened. But isn't that just how Washington works? Bob Packwood drew some terrible press in the famous Philadelphia Inquirer series of articles that led to Barlett and Steele's two best-selling books, "America. What Went Wrong?" and "America. Who Really Pays the Taxes?" The authors made it pretty clear that Packwood had added riders to tax bills to favor specific people who had contributed to his campaigns. And, of course, everyone knows that lobbyists and PACs are *in the business* of giving money to candidates to gain access and to try to win their help later.

3. What Gale humorously referred to as the "Star Fuckers". These are people who want to be able to say, "Yeah, I helped put Harry Lonsdale in office. He's a personal friend of mine." More than the other groups, these people have to be convinced you're going to win. So, the polling results are especially important to them. Your friends will likely give you money no matter what the polls say, and PACs frequently grease both sides.

So, it's a "Catch 22" situation: you have to have enough money to be a viable candidate to be able to raise more money—enough to win.

James Carville may have been right when he advised presidential candidate Bill Clinton in 1992, "It's the economy, stupid!", because he knew that Clinton had, or could raise, enough money to be competitive. But for most candidates—not incumbents, of course—"It's the *money*, stupid!"

# # #

I never knew there were so many ways of saying "no," without actually uttering the word. Nor so many apparently valid reasons for saying "no." But here's a tiny fraction of the responses I received when I was dialing for dollars:

> I have 3 kids in college...
> I just lost my job...
> We're just back from vacation, and we're a little flat right now...
> My daughter is getting married next weekend...
> I'm having a hip replacement on Thursday...
> I'm maxed out...
> We've just bought a new twin-engine airplane...
> I'm broke...
> I've never contributed to a politician in my life...
> I'll have to talk it over with my spouse... (50% of the prospects used this one.)
> I just made my quarterly income tax payment and...
> I'm not sure. Let me think about it ... (a guaranteed, if delayed, "no")
> I'll see what I can do ... (another guaranteed "no")
> I'm supporting your opponent!

On the other hand, some people are incredibly generous. I didn't need to apply heavy pressure to them (bless their hearts, because I hated to). Some were friends, of course, but some were strangers and I wondered why they did it. Many people in this country are conditioned to give to political candidates. You just have to be from the right party, be right on a key issue or two, and *ask*. You almost always have to *ask*.

But I won't forget Janet Tobkin. She was a tree-hugger and she knew that I was, too, but we had never met. One day, she walked into our downtown Portland headquarters and said to me, "Harry I don't have any money, but I could sell my old beater of a car, probably for $600, and contribute the money to your campaign. I can start taking the bus to work." We refused her offer, but it sure was motivating.

I had been coached to ask for a specific amount of money in my fund-raising efforts. But *what* amount? You need to know, according to the experts like Scott Gale, their *ability* to give. But how are you supposed to know that? Gale says that no one is ever insulted by your asking for too much. They may not be insulted, but there's sure a hiatus in the conversation as they suck in air when you ask for the maximum of $1000.

But I'm in no position to complain. Before I ran myself in 1990, I don't think I'd ever given any candidate more than $100, and I'd rarely given anybody *anything*. And I'd even more rarely been asked. I won't forget a phone call I received once from Congressman Ron Wyden. Wyden then sat on the House Small Business Committee. I had attended a couple of his small business meetings in Bend and Portland. There was a sign-up sheet, and I naively wondered why. When he later phoned me, he rattled on for a good 10 minutes, talking about every issue under the sun, asking for my opinion. Then he moved in for the kill and asked me for a $1000 contribution. I couldn't believe it. Sucked air. Told him "no", pure and simple.

Then there was the Oregon Business Council. This is a collection of forty or so of Oregon's heavyweight business people: presidents or CEOs of the banks, utilities, major industries and—for three years or so—*me*. I got out my trusty list of OBC members and their alternates, another forty people. That's maybe eighty people, total. I called them all except two, the two biggest "timber beasts". I figured that asking *them* for money for my campaign would surely be a waste of time. I only reached about eight people, leaving messages with secretaries to the other seventy. A handful called back. Not one contributed so much as a dime. Only one had the guts to tell me he wasn't contributing, but supporting Hatfield instead.

Of all the people I called —several thousand —it was true that almost all of them could have sent me a $100 or even a $1000 check that day and "not missed lunch the next day", to quote Scott Gale. But most didn't. Just like I hadn't.

One of the true unpleasantries in making fund-raising phone calls was all of those unreturned phone messages I left with people all across Oregon and around the country. As a small businessman, it was my practice to return all of the calls made to me, usually within 24 hours, if I wasn't out of the country. I made exceptions, of course. Insurance salespersons, stockbrokers making cold-calls who wanted me to invest in some hot new issue, and a few others did not get their calls returned — once my secretary or I was able to identify them. But everyone else, even including some cranks and pests, did.

I would guess that at least 80% of my "left messages" were never returned, even many of those to friends, some of whom are now ex-friends. There was one guy, a man I had helped professionally on more than one occasion, to whom I placed no less than ten phone calls—for money, of course—that I was never able to reach. To him, I had become an insurance salesman! Saying "no" is hard, and some of us will go to great lengths to avoid it.

And then there are those who say "yes" to everyone. Someone on our staff took it upon himself to check Mark Hatfield's contributors. He found that a few Hatfield contributors had also sent a check to us! One of those people was Ray Steinfeld, who runs a successful food-processing business in Oregon. Try as I might I couldn't find any reason for someone to write a check to two opposing candidates than this one: he was buying access to the winner. But should access be for sale? Did any of my contributors think they were buying access to me? (We returned all checks to those people who we detected were playing both sides.)

We raised money every which way we could, as long as it was ethical. The Federal Election Commission's fund raising rules being what they are, if it's ethical, it's better than legal. We sold "Lonsdale for Senate" lapel buttons and bumper stickers for a buck a piece. We held several successful auctions and even hired a professional auctioneer and brought in celebrities like environmentalists David Brower or Denis Hayes as draws. We tried running a TV spot with an 800 telephone number that could be called to make a money pledge. It was a bust; we brought in maybe 10% of the cost of the ad. We sent out *hundreds of thousands* of fund-raising letters to targeted groups, each with a remittance envelope. I traveled to the homes of Democrats from Manhattan to Beverly Hills and from Medford to Astoria with my "tin cup". I was once scheduled to meet with constituents (read, "raise money") on the Oregon coast, but we were stranded in Portland by the ice storm of the century. So we did it by speaker phone in the home of the hostess, Jean Harmon. We raised over $1000, a lot by our standards, without my even showing up, thanks to some hard work by the hostess and her friends.

Every fund-raising party we held, of course, ended with the money pitch, either by the candidate or by Kris Rees or Mitzi Scott (or Bill Kemp, our volunteer fund-raiser in '96), all of whom were much better at it than I. Oregon is the only state in the country, I believe, where individuals can contribute $50 per year—that's $200 for a married couple every two-year election cycle—to the candidate of their choice, and get the entire contribution back in their next state income tax return. It continually surprised me how few people would even contribute a free $50. Most people came to these fund raisers to meet the candidate and shake his hand and make a personal appraisal. More than a few came to vent their anger at the politicians back in Washington, D.C. They'd complain to *me* for things that Mark Hatfield or Bob Packwood or Jesse Helms or George Bush (the elder) or Ronald Reagan had done!

I found that it's especially hard to raise campaign contributions if you're perceived as being rich. The Oregonian and the state's other media outlets had repeatedly and incorrectly described me as a "multimillionaire," in spite of my many attempts to correct that error. There's a dichotomy: most Democrats, at least, don't like the idea of Congress being filled with a bunch of millionaires, people who are presumed to be out of touch with the common man. And so millionaires are expected to fund their own campaigns. My own take is that it is vastly better to have a multimillionaire in the Senate, someone who presumably wouldn't try to pull any shenanigans to line her or his pocket, than to have a bunch of "PAC rats" there, who will do the PAC's bidding to assure their re-election.

We once held a fund raiser at the home of some business friends in Bend. About 50 invited people were confirmed attendees, many of them friends. But a few days before the event, the host told me they had received a phone call from a lumber broker in town by the name of Loren Irving who knew of my strong environmental positions. He threatened my friends, the hosts, with economic reprisals if they held the fund raiser. And so we had the event, but it *wasn't* a fund raiser. Now, the wife of the lumber broker happened to be the owner of my favorite bookstore in Bend. I was so peeved at her husband's high-handed behavior that I confronted her with the story at my next opportunity. I now buy my books elsewhere.

Not every fund raiser started out as a fund raiser. The friendly little town of Rogue River, Oregon, population 2000, is nestled alongside the river it is named after, which is one of America's finest rafting, fishing, and hiking rivers. Rogue River is a timber town, and the mill there, then owned by Medite Corp., employed 50-60 people during the good times. But things have been changing there, too. The mill has been shut down periodically, sometimes for months at a time. In those times, unemployment soars, and the town is in the dumps.

But a new breed of folks have come to Rogue River, just as they have to so many timber towns in the West: the retired and the entrepreneurs who see opportunity in almost anything, from high tech to sandwich shops.

We had an event scheduled in Rogue River one relatively lazy Sunday afternoon. We met in the Grange hall. And we had a huge crowd — close to 200 people — more, in fact, than most of our Portland events drew.

Who were these people, I asked myself, and why have they come out here today to hear *me*? You learn it all, in the Q. and A. session. First, I learned that they were a very friendly crowd, unlike some I had confronted in timber towns. And the thrust of the group, the main reason most of them had come out, was that they wanted something more for their town than the boom-and-bust of the milltown economy. I offered them some hope that their town, with its exquisite setting, could thrive and maybe even grow without cutting down every tree within twenty miles. My hometown of Bend had done just that.

Whoever organized the event did not describe it to us as a "money" event, meaning that I wasn't supposed to put on my money pitch at the end. And I didn't. But as things were winding down, some guy from the back of the room came forward, took one of the straight-back chairs that wasn't in use, took out his wallet and pulled out a $20 bill. He folded it in half and draped it over the back of the chair, with these words: "I think we ought to help elect this guy. He thinks like we do. He'll need money. I want somebody here to match my twenty bucks." There was a precious moment or two of surprise and inaction around the room. Then a second man stood up and said, "I ain't got twenty but here's five." And he draped his folded bill over the back of the chair. And the floodgates opened. A few ones, another five, a ten, another twenty. Although it was already late, we all hung around and started talking — not the canned talk, just talk.

We walked out of there with $320 in cash, and some new friends. I won't forget Rogue River.

# # #

Sundays and evenings were the best times for fund raisers, and we did as many as we could schedule, sometimes three a day. As in all things campaign-wise, there's no such thing as a "typical" fund raiser. Each one was a new experience. But some things were common to all.

"Where the heck *is* this place, Kris? We're late *again*. Will anybody still be there? This street isn't even shown on the Portland city map. And how can the house numbers jump from the 300s to the 8000s, in one block? Oh, I get it. We left Beaverton and now we're in Hillsboro — or someplace. And what are the names of the host and hostess? Am I supposed to know them?"

"You met them last week at the Smiths'. She's Sierra Club, tree-hugger, he's a lawyer, but not your typical lawyer."

"Boy, am I pooped! And hungry. What time is it?"

"Relax, Harry, we're here. At least this looks like the place. Cars out front. The light's on. Will this rain *ever* stop?! Your hair's a mess. Loosen your tie, but don't take it off, and roll up your sleeves. I'll do the money pitch."

"Oh, hi, Allene; hi, Fred. It's *so* good of you to host this thing. I'm sorry we're so late. Traffic..."

Then follows about an hour of being introduced to everyone there, even the dog; making small-talk with the folks; trying to snatch a few of those shrimp before they're all gone. Thoughts: Oh, god, look at that incredible cherry cheesecake for dessert. Must remember to find an excuse to get back to this table after the money pitch, but before we leave. Trying desperately to remember all the names, and failing again, miserably. Five names, I might remember all five. Ten names, I might remember three. *Thirty* names, I remember *zero*, nada, zip. Why do I even try? Jeez, don't forget the host's and hostess's names, whatever you do, knucklehead!

The stump speech. "Hello, I'm Harry Lonsdale, and I'm so glad you've taken the time to come out this rainy evening. And I'm so grateful to Allene and Fred (whew!) for opening up their home and for putting this event together. I know it's a lot of work..."

The pitch. Scientist, businessman, entrepreneur, high tech company in Bend, environmentalist, forests, women's rights, the changing economy, choice, Hatfield, Washington, D.C., corruption, we can fix it ... over, and over, and over.

Searching the faces for clues as to what will sell to this audience. Hoping for a leading question, from which to launch into some aspect in greater detail.

First question. Polite. Intelligent. A softball, right down the middle. I shine.

Second question. Off the wall. How do I feel about tykittyporn? About *what*? "You know, tykittyporn. The importation of pornographic videos from Thailand that they're selling to kids!"

"Oh! Thai kiddy porn!"

How to respond?

"I'm against."

Next question. Nasty. Personal. Who invited *him*? Keep *cool*. Respond.

Next question. Some guy making a speech about the forests, or the economy, or Nike exploitation of Indonesian workers, or drugs-and-why-we-should-decriminalize-them, or solar energy, or *whatever*. Let him ramble on. Agree with him if you can. Finally, try to cut him off and get back on track. *I* am the one who's running, after all! Lots of concerned and informed people ask good questions that give me an opportunity to explain my positions.

Next question. Next. Next ...

Finally, the money pitch. I'm almost done for now. What time is it? Anything else scheduled this evening?

"Now, I'd like to introduce my good friend Kris Rees. Kris quit her job in Bend to help me on this campaign, and I hope you'll give her your attention for a few minutes."

"Yes, that's true, and let me tell you why I quit my job to sign on" ... praise for Harry ... let's help elect Harry ... Harry needs money ... the first $50 is fully refundable ... television ads are expensive ... do you want six more years of Mark Hatfield and his terrible environmental policies? ... just skip one dinner for two ... money ... Money ... *MONEY!*

Chit chat. Press the flesh, again. Avoid the asshole with the nasty question. Thank the host and hostess again. Damn! All the cherry cheesecake is gone. Out the door, through the rain, to the car. Count the money! $650. Not bad. "Good job, Kris. You knocked 'em dead."

"You were good, too, but you look tired. Dan Walter's here to take you to your next fund raiser. I'll see you tomorrow morning. Get some rest!"

"Hey, Dan!"

"Hey, Ace, how's it going?"

Back to Interstate 5, in search of the next fund-raising event. More of the same. Finally, around 10 p.m. our work for the day was over and it was onward to some Motel 6 for the night. More rain. Bed. Pull the covers over my head. "They can't get me in here." Blessed sleep.

And so it went.

Toward the end of the Hatfield campaign in 1990, we expected the Democratic Senatorial Campaign Committee (DSCC) to provide some financial help. I never knew just where the DSCC raised its money, nor how they raised it. Frankly, I didn't *want* to know. All I knew was that the DSCC was allowed under Federal Election Commission rules to contribute a prescribed amount of money to candidate races—not to the candidate herself or himself, but to buy TV time with, for example. The amount of money was fixed by the population of the state; for Oregon, it came to something over $200,000: a *lot* of money. And since we had a contested race, and I was doing reasonably well in the polls in October, I expected that money. But they made me beg. Actually, what they wanted was for me to call my rich friends (*what* rich friends?) and get them to write a check to the DSCC for up to $25,000, the legal limit, before they would release the $200,000+ to our campaign.

Not only did I know *very* few people with a disposable $25,000, of the few I knew no one wanted to contribute that kind of money to the Democratic Party, in which many of my friends had lost confidence. So I struck out. The DSCC persisted. I finally turned to the one source that I knew couldn't say "no" to me: my *mom*. Now, this whole fund-raising gutter is bad enough with strangers or even with friends. Anyone with an ounce of dignity or self respect would rather slash their wrists than get on the phone to ask for money. But to ask one's own mother was the final indignity. I asked. To my mother, who lived through the Depression, a dollar tip in a restaurant was too much. Finally, she wrote the DSCC a check for $15,000; I hung my head, and they bought $217,000 worth of TV advertising.

With all of that, with more than 5000 fund-raising calls in 1990 from me alone, with countless events and other money-raising gimmicks, we still didn't have enough money in the final stages of the Hatfield campaign. Hatfield raised and spent $2.7 million, much of it from PACs and other out-of-state sources; we raised and spent $1.4 million, $800,000 of it mine, $200,000 from the DSCC, and the rest from the 5000 contributors. His TV barrage in the closing days was decisive. I won't forget his hourly TV spots in Bend, all day every day.

Being outspent by Hatfield by a ratio of two to one might have been decisive; his incumbency was probably worth even more than the money. Being outspent by AuCoin by three to one, and by Bruggere by ten to one clearly *was* decisive. And I outspent my Democratic opponents in the 1990 primary by a wide margin. There has got to be a better way to fund election campaigns, and I will turn to that subject in the final chapter.

Harry Lonsdale

CHAPTER 6.

THE PRESS

Among the cornerstones of the American way of life are freedom of speech and freedom of the press. Both were guaranteed in the First Amendment to our Constitution, with these words: "Congress shall make no law ... abridging the freedom of speech, or of the press ... ." The Founding Fathers correctly perceived that those two freedoms are essential to all of the other freedoms we enjoy. In spite of many challenges over the years, the Supreme Court has vigorously defended those freedoms, and we can all be thankful that they have. What must it be like to live in a country where the government controls the media and to go through an entire lifetime and never really know the truth about what's going on in one's own country or around the world?

Not only do our U.S. newspapers bring us reasonably accurate news, but they do it surprisingly inexpensively. For something like 50 cents a day, even small town newspapers bring us information that it would simply be impossible for us to gather individually on our own. And not only do our 50-odd cable TV channels bring us virtually instantaneous action pictures of what's of interest around the globe, they do it for a few pennies a day worth of electricity and our monthly cable bill.

There's a lot more to like about the press. Thanks to the Freedom of Information Act and the kind of investigative journalism now pursued by some reporters, there's little that the American public can't find out about just by picking up the newspaper. Without the persistence and shoe leather of Woodward and Bernstein of The Washington Post, the Watergate scandal would never have happened. And the inevitable leaks that every administration complains about (but, thankfully, can't stop) are a factor in keeping our elected officials accountable.

Every time our country is engaged in a military action, there's no shortage of reporters eager to cover it, right up to the front lines, in spite of the risk. An important job of the military in recent years has been to keep the press *away* from the action.

Many an honorable reporter has suffered the consequences—even jail time—of refusing to reveal their sources when under court order to do so.

And how many journalists in foreign lands have been murdered or imprisoned for attempting to report the news or their views? Yes, there is much to admire about the press.

But if our free press is so great, why do so many people in public office, even those with the greatest integrity, hate it so? And, more importantly, why have we as a nation come to increasingly distrust the press? Finally, why am I devoting a chapter in this book to the press?

Those are difficult questions, and a number of people more knowledgeable than I have offered answers. Some of their comments can be found in the "Media" section of the Bibliography. But here's my take: it's a matter of accountability, or lack of same. We've protected press freedom so diligently that that freedom has turned to *un*-accountability which has turned to arrogance. No, not everywhere, everyone, or all the time, but often enough.

# # #

One can gain some appreciation of the dichotomy of our feelings, as a nation, toward the press by examining the words of Thomas Jefferson. Here is what that Prince of Americans had to say about the press in 1786:

"Our liberty depends on the freedom of the press, and that cannot be limited without being lost."

And in 1787, he wrote these stirring and frequently quoted words:

"...were it left to me to decide whether we should have a government without newspapers, or newspapers without a government, I should not hesitate for a moment to prefer the latter."

Now, let's turn to what Jefferson had to say about the press in 1807, when he was in his second term as president:

"Nothing can now be believed which is seen in a newspaper. Truth itself becomes suspicious by being put into that polluted vehicle."

And further, in 1807:

"The man who never looks into a newspaper is better informed than he who reads them: in as much as he who knows nothing is nearer to truth than he whose mind is filled with falsehood and errors."

And still further, in 1807:

"Perhaps an editor might begin a reformation in some such way as this. Divide his paper into four chapters, heading the first, Truths. 2nd, Probabilities. 3rd, Possibilities. 4th, Lies. The first chapter would be very short."

So how could this brilliant man, who found the press so essential in 1786 find it so reprehensible 20 years later? Could it be the result of several years of being pummeled in his role as president by the nation's newspaper editors?

This love-hate relationship with the press has transcended the years. Here are some further quotes, from some people who should have known:

John Swinton, 1830-1901, editor, New York Sun, "There is no such thing as an independent press in America. ... "We are the tools and vassals of the rich men behind the scenes ... We are intellectual prostitutes."

E.W. Scripps, 1854-1926, press baron, "In America, the press rules the country; it rules its politics, its religion, its social practices ... The press of this country is now and always has been so thoroughly dominated by the wealthy few of the country that it cannot be depended upon to give the great mass of the people that correct information concerning political, economical, and social subjects which it is necessary that the mass of the people shall have, in order that they shall vote and in all ways act in the best way to protect themselves from the brutal force and the chicanery of the ruling and employing class."

American writer Theodore Dreiser, 1871-1945, "The American press, with a very few exceptions, is a kept press. Kept by the big corporations the way a whore is kept by a rich man."

Alexander Solzhenitsyn, 1918-, Russian writer, "...the press has become the greatest power within the Western countries, more powerful than the legislature, the executive, and the judiciary."

And, finally and currently, a local newspaperman, Doug Bates, former managing editor of The (Eugene) Register-Guard, and former general news editor of The Seattle Times, "...the assumption that newspapers are bastions of tolerant, broad-minded, liberal values ... is a myth. In reality, the newspaper industry ranks among the most conservative, change-resistant, and bias-prone institutions in the United States." (from "The Pulitzer Prize," Birch Lane Press, New York, 1991).

Is this the same press that Thomas Jefferson wrote so glowingly about in 1786?

The quotes above refer to press bias, press lies, press ownership by the wealthy, even press whores. There's probably some truth in all of those charges. But I want to focus on another aspect: press arrogance, particularly as it is exemplified by newspaper editors.

One of the many tests of our freedom of the press resulted in an important U.S. Supreme Court decision in 1964 known as *New York Times vs. Sullivan*. The Court decided in that case that in order to be found guilty of libel the author of a newspaper story or editorial had to *knowingly* print a false and damaging statement against a public figure. It isn't enough that the statement is false and damaging, it also had to be the intent of the newspaper to print it *knowing* that it was false. Obviously, there's a difficult burden of proof required of the libeled person. And that decision has given great protection and comfort to people working in the print press. It applies, as noted, only to "public figures," but that definition includes every sports figure or movie star or entertainer or elected official or candidate or hero or villain you've ever heard of, and a lot more that you haven't.

The bottom line is that the press has been afforded more than adequate protection from those who would curb its independence. That protection has bred arrogance.

#

The late Bob Chandler owned and ran my hometown paper, The (Bend) Bulletin for about 40 years. Bob and I had a long-term feud going all the years I knew him, although I will confess that he won every public engagement, since he bought his ink by the barrel. After suffering through one too many of his opinion pieces in the paper, I wrote him a letter about whatever it was that he had irritated me with that day, and I managed to insert a reference to the famous quote from Mark Twain, "He was as arrogant as a small-town newspaper editor." That little quip cemented two decades of enmity.

Another time I took exception to something Chandler had editorialized about and I tried to write a rebuttal. Chandler rejected it. So I tried to buy some space in the paper for my rebuttal. That didn't work either, because Chandler wouldn't print my ad. When I called him about it he informed me of the facts: no newspaper is forced to print something that they don't want to print, regardless of the fact that it didn't contain anything libelous, obscene, untrue, or threatening.

When I was running for office, Chandler printed an opinion piece about me that I felt was both untrue and insulting. I felt that, even though I couldn't stand this guy, I should make an effort to patch things up. So I invited him to lunch, and he accepted.

We went to a little Italian restaurant in town and sat in a booth, facing one another. After the usual pleasantries—pretty scant, that day—and after we had ordered our meals, I pulled out the editorial about me and said, "Bob, how would you like it if I said these words about *you*, in your newspaper?" Chandler stood up, threw down his napkin, and said, "I knew you'd come here with a hard-on. (Now shouting) Waitress! I'll take my meal in the next booth!" That was the last time I ever spoke with him.

#

The news and the advertisements fill up the major part of any newspaper. But, for many of us, it's the third part, the *opinion* part of the newspaper — comprised of editorials, columns, op-eds, and letters to the editor — that's the most interesting. Letters to the editor are my favorite part of any newspaper, and I'm grateful that editors allow us to have our say, even though they put limits on how much space we are granted and on how frequently we can submit articles. The letters-to-the-editor section is "America Speaking," and amid the din and the complaints and the occasional wackiness can frequently be found as much wisdom and clear thinking as is to be found anywhere.

One reason to appreciate letters to the editor and op-eds is that they are signed by the author. That one, seemingly small element, the name of the author, is important. Because the writer can't hide behind anonymity, he or she is frequently more polite, more fair, and even more reasoned.

It's in the editorials that newspapers (read "editorial page editors") demonstrate their arrogance, and that derives in large part from the fact that those editorials, in almost every U.S. newspaper, are unsigned. What freedom those editors have! First, they can say whatever they want — protected by the First Amendment and *N.Y. Times vs. Sullivan* — screw anyone they please, and get away with it. No one, except the publisher and perhaps a handful of insiders at the paper, even knows who those editorial writers are. When we write a *signed* letter to the editor, we have to be careful to exhibit at least a little civility — or the target of our remarks can fight back with her or his rebuttal in the same newspaper.

But editorial writers have no fear of any of that. If they insult someone or make a major boo-boo, the worst that will happen to them is to see a letter submitted reading something like, "The author of an editorial in the August 12 edition of the Post is wrong when he or she says..." It's totally impersonal; there's no pain. And, if the editor chooses to, he or she can rebut the author of the letter-to-the-editor, by name, till the cows come home!

Newspaper editors thus have a great deal of power over the people they write about, and with essentially no accountability. Most of us who work for a living are accountable to *someone*: there's always a superior, a bottom line, or a board of directors. Work itself, I've always thought, is any kind of physical or mental activity with *accountability*. Without it, you're just playing or recreating.

Harry Lonsdale

To some extent, a newspaper editor has a boss, unless the editor owns the paper. But, to the audience that really counts, — the readers — those anonymous editorial writers are unaccountable.

And so I have been waging a campaign — it seems like a one-man campaign, thus far — to get newspaper editors to sign their editorials. Why don't they? Here are some of the excuses I've heard: "It's not the newspaper's policy." "Too many people would have to sign off." "Some of our editorial board members take exception to some of, or some part of, our editorials." Blah, blah, blah. What they really mean is, "We're chicken! We don't want to take the heat; we just want to dish it out." Signed editorials wouldn't automatically bring about humility in editors. But it would be a step in the right direction.

# # #

The Perot run for the Presidency in 1992 was a breath of fresh air for millions of Americans. Here was a guy, fed up with politics as usual and with enough money to challenge the system. Unlike so many other wealthy whiners about government, he put his money where his mouth was. Whatever else we may think about Ross the Boss, we're indebted to him for making the effort and for exposing some of the hypocrisy and corruption back in Washington, D.C.

We're all in his debt, if for no other reason than the fact that he took on the arrogant press ... with his *own* arrogance. It was predictable that this proud, cock-sure, independent man from Texas would clash with the press, to his own undoing. A new expression came out of his 1992 campaign, "gotcha journalism". It was coined, apparently, by Perot himself. And it was so fitting.

Perot may or may not have been an egomaniac. But he was certainly thin-skinned for someone who wanted to be president. And that's probably why he's now happily out of politics: he couldn't take the heat.

There's usually someone on the staff of every major American newspaper assigned to the "attack dog" function. At The Oregonian, for years that choice role fell to columnist and ex-sportswriter Steve Duin. At the Salem Statesman Journal, it was a jolly but deadly man named Ron Blankenbaker, a columnist. At The (Eugene) Register-Guard, it was reporter Brent Walth. Those guys were meat eaters, and candidates were their favorite meat. The management at many newspapers obviously encourage these "attack dogs." Their columns are widely read, because most of us enjoy reading about the foibles of our public figures, especially about politicians.

Their style goes something like this. Instead of saying that "Senate candidate Harry Lonsdale laid out his proposal for balancing the national budget at a press conference in Portland yesterday. His proposal would increase taxes on the rich and on corporations...," they would offer something along these lines: "Multimillionaire Senate candidate Harry Lonsdale, obviously pandering to labor unions, again demonstrated his arrogance and soft-headedness at a press conference in Portland yesterday. Is this bozo really serious?..."

I found that these "attack dogs" reserved their best stuff for challengers, and especially for political unknowns. They pulled their punches with incumbents. They knew that challengers probably weren't going to be successful—more than 90% and sometimes 98% of incumbent Congresspersons are returned to office—and so it was safe to pummel the challengers. To be nasty to an incumbent means risking the loss of precious access in the future.

My attitude toward difficult people like these, back when I was in the business world, was to try to disarm them by taking them to lunch—mostly so that they could see that I was an ordinary person, just like themselves. And I did take both Duin and Blankenbaker to lunch, at different times. I remember telling each of them—not referring exclusively to myself and how I felt they had demeaned me—"You know Steve/Ron, these people you write about in your columns, these are *real* people, with real friends and real families. And real feelings. Speaking for myself, when I go shopping at Safeway, or go to my barbershop for a haircut, or fill up my gas tank at my regular gas station, I ask myself, 'Does this person I'm dealing with read Steve Duin's column? Do they think that those awful things that Steve says about me are *true*? I sure hope not!'" But my pleas got me nowhere. When you're the candidate, you're the meat.

Ross Perot understands, no doubt. Even Thomas Jefferson came to understand.

This issue is about more than Harry Lonsdale or any one candidate for office. The "attack dogs" typically fill their columns with innuendo and exaggeration rather than cold facts (or even a fairly presented but contrary opinion). These daily attacks over a period of months and years contribute to the public's distrust of their elected representatives and their government. I am not protesting against criticism of politicians, but rather the nasty columns that devalue their subjects just for the entertainment value of the column. They're tearing down America. When they subsequently complain about "Americans not voting," they can look to their own handiwork.

# # #

I've already cited the fact that just two days prior to the May 1992 Democratic primary, in which we lost to Les AuCoin, The Oregonian, in repeating their AuCoin endorsement, editorialized that "Harry Lonsdale has run a low and dishonest campaign." We were bewildered by that statement. It was too late to even attempt any damage control. We just had to seethe in frustration.

Career politicians no doubt would have simply shrugged that insult off. Most have suffered a lot worse. But I tried to pursue the matter after the election. Why, I wondered, would the paper describe me as dishonest, and what could I do about it? Why should I even care—the election was over and we had lost, right? But reputations are important. I had spent 60+ years building mine—we ran on a campaign of integrity, after all—and, once lost, it's hard to get one's reputation back. I could have spared myself the effort.

First, I tried to call the editorial page editor, a man named Bob Landauer, whom I knew slightly. He wouldn't return my phone calls. Who else to turn to? It turns out that many newspapers in America subscribe to something called a news council, a place where complainants like me can take their beefs. The Oregonian subscribes to one called the Northwest News Council, located on the campus of the University of Washington in Seattle, and run by an affable man named Oren Campbell. Campbell heard my story, and wrote to The Oregonian's publisher, then a man named Bill Hilliard, whom I did not know. Hilliard simply brushed off Campbell and his news council. All he said in his perfunctory response to Campbell was, no, they would not meet to discuss my complaint. But he added gratuitously that "Mr. Lonsdale has never failed to take any complaints directly to me" (Hilliard) ... which was absolute bunk.

The whole affair stank so bad that even Bob Chandler, owner and editor of The (Bend) Bulletin and certainly no friend of mine, rose up in disgust. In an opinion piece with the headline "News/Arrogance a Bitter Pill", Chandler penned [The Bulletin, March 14, 1993]: "But I do think Bill Hilliard erred when he would neither return telephone calls nor respond to a written request from the council [the Northwest News Council]..." "The council was, to put it mildly, outraged when Hilliard would not respond. In its public report to those interested it said 'Either The Oregonian has adopted an attitude of total arrogance or it is unwilling to place its trust in a journalism news council...'"

Chandler went on, "The question which comes quickly to my mind is this: How can The Oregonian complain so loudly about Bob Packwood's refusal to meet with its reporters when its own editor adamantly refuses to even discuss a complaint that he has his facts wrong ...?" Interestingly, that's exactly what I thought Chandler had done to *me*, previously.

Too bad that no one in Portland reads The Bulletin. And Bill Hilliard was no misfit: the American Society of Newspaper Editors elected him as their president at about that time.

What was left for me to do to rectify the injustice? Virtually out of options, I learned of the Columbia Journalism Review, a periodical produced by the Journalism School at Columbia University. They regularly include a section entitled "Darts and Laurels", wherein they praise people and organizations for jobs well done and criticize those that screw up. We wrote to them with our story and they awarded The Oregonian a Dart, for not participating in the complaint process, which provided at least a minimum of satisfaction. But how many Oregonians ever saw the Dart, or ever knew the story behind it?

# # #

None of the newspapers in eastern Oregon is more conservative than the Wallowa County Chieftain, a tiny local paper in the small, lovely town of Enterprise, Oregon, population 2000. The Chieftain has been the subject of several defamation lawsuits in recent years, gaining them an unflattering article in The Oregonian as well as a damning television documentary piece on one of the Portland TV channels (for which they unsuccessfully sued the TV station).

The newspaper is a family affair. The editor is Rick Swart; his father, Donald, is the publisher; and the founder, before the turn of the 20th century, was Donald's father.

In the heat of the '92 AuCoin campaign, my friend in Wallowa County, Ric Bailey, faxed us an editorial written by Rick Swart with the headline, "Harry Lies". Yes, *this* Harry.

The genesis of the article was a long standing feud between jet boaters and rafters on the Snake River in Hell's Canyon. A jet boat is a high powered, very noisy, shallow draft and very fast boat that is used to take sight-seeing vacationers into the interior of Hell's Canyon. In and out, the whole trip takes less than half a day. It's a profitable business for a few Idahoans. The rafters are an entirely different breed. They normally take three or four days or more to quietly drift through the canyon, making camp each evening with their guests. Ric Bailey is one of the rafting concessionaires, and the float trip I took with him in 1991 indirectly led to Swart's editorial.

It seems that one Dennis Gratton, a jet-boat operator and an enemy of Ric Bailey's, was hiding in the bushes with his camcorder at one of our campsites on our float trip. (No, I'm not making this up!) Gratton hoped to get some embarrassing videotape of our doings to publicly embarrass Bailey, presumably out of revenge. Gratton videotaped for several hours that evening, captured nothing untoward, but reported to Swart that our encampment was a drunken bacchanal, with pot-smoking, booze, nudity, and "howling at the moon". He also reported that I was part of the group. That part, at least, was true.

Swart then called our Senate campaign office in Portland to confirm that I was, indeed, on the trip. I was on the road the day he called and he spoke with our press secretary, a very capable woman named Kathy McShea. At the time of the float trip, I had not even met Kathy, who is a professional journalist from Washington D.C. Swart described the trip in the most earthy (and incorrect) terms and asked Kathy if I was on the trip. She, of course, had no way of knowing what I was doing some months before she and I had even met, but based on Swart's gross description, she responded that I couldn't possibly have been on such a trip. Swart took that as a denial from me and let his poison pen do the rest. What resulted was a total smear.

When we received a fax of the article from Bailey, we immediately called Swart in Enterprise, and demanded a retraction of the article, and

Swart agreed to do the retraction. But the next edition of the weekly paper had an equally damaging editorial by Swart under the headline "Caught in a Web," the thrust of which was that I first denied being on the now infamous float trip, and then when "caught red-handed", had admitted it. (Between the two editorials, Swart had attended my debate with AuCoin in Pendleton. When the debate was over he approached me—I didn't know who he was—and asked if I had been on a float trip with Ric Bailey the previous summer. I told him I had, of course.)

So now we have two newspaper articles calling me a liar. Admittedly, they were in one of the most obscure papers in Oregon but lies in print hurt and have a way of becoming truths, if not corrected. We later learned that AuCoin was trying desperately to have the articles run in other Oregon newspapers. Wisely, they all turned him down.

After another round of angry phone calls to Swart from which we got no satisfaction, we felt we had no recourse but to sue Swart and this newspaper for defamation.

The last thing I needed at the end of a hotly contested Senate primary campaign was a lawsuit. But it's always been my belief that when you're wronged you should fight back, whatever the consequences. I remember asking myself, "Is this, too, part of running for office?!"

We found a very competent defamation attorney in David Force of Eugene. Among his credits, Force had represented clients who successfully sued both The Oregonian and The (Bend) Bulletin for defamation.

But things did not go well for us in the courts. Our first move was to try for a change of venue, to prevent the possibility of a home-town decision. That attempt failed; the case was heard by a judge in eastern Oregon, and we lost. We then appealed the decision to the Oregon Court of Appeals. I was present when Force and the Chieftain's attorney presented their oral arguments to a three-member panel of the Appeals Court. At the end of the arguments, I was convinced, based on the questions posed by the court and the performances of the two attorneys, that we had successfully gained a reversal. Force felt so, too, and the opposing attorney showed every sign as we walked out of the courtroom that he thought so, too.

Wrong. In a 2-1 decision, the Appeals Court did *not* reverse. We then appealed to the Oregon Supreme Court which, after many months, let stand the lower court's decision. We lost.

Harry Lonsdale

Along the way, a Portland TV station had asked me to appear to talk about the Chieftain and its record of drawing defamation lawsuits. I was pleased to do so, and described how Swart's headline "Harry Lies" was itself a lie. As a result of which we found *ourselves* the target of the Chieftain's defamation suit! We had sued them for $500,000 — a limit pushed through the Oregon legislature years ago by the state's newspapers — and they sued us for $800,000! There's no legal limit in Oregon when an individual, as opposed to a newspaper, is sued for defamation. Their suit was pure intimidation, of course, and they made us an offer to drop their suit if we dropped ours — one of the oldest tricks in the lawyer's bag. We didn't drop ours, but they eventually dropped theirs.

Years later, I received a letter from Rick Swart, apologizing for his earlier behavior and for all the pain he had caused me. He admitted to having been a long-term alcoholic and to having done some damaging things to a number of other people as a result of his disease. His admission was actually part of his recovery treatment but, still, it was a noble thing to do.

I have inserted this long and tedious story to bring out the following point. The protections granted to our nation's newspapers by the First Amendment and the Supreme Court's *New York Times vs. Sullivan* decision are awesome. Ordinary citizens have considerable protection against libel. If someone calls you a whore in print, and you aren't one, you can sue and you'll probably win. Public figures — and I was one as a result of my 1990 Senate campaign — have no such protection. Under the *New York Times* decision, if a newspaper calls a public figure a whore and *knows that the public figure isn't*, that's libel. But who can prove what the editor knew when he/she wrote something?

It isn't just editorial writers who have virtual immunity from defamation charges regarding public figures. It's every reporter, columnist, talk-show host, and political cartoonist; in actuality, it's *any*one.

I'm reminded of Vince Foster's suicide note. Foster was President Clinton's friend and deputy legal counsel, and he shot himself in the head in a park outside Washington, D.C., in 1993. Suicide is usually a complex issue, and we may never know the totality of Foster's reasons. But shortly before he ended his life, he was the object of some stinging personal attacks in editorials in The Wall St. Journal. He wrote these words in his brief suicide note: "The WSJ editors lie without consequence. I was not meant for the job or the spotlight of public life in Washington. Here, ruining people is considered sport."

The Supreme Court has made bad decisions in the past. Most recently, there was the flagrantly political decision in *Bush vs. Gore* in 2000. Much earlier, they decided that slavery was O.K. in the Dred Scott decision in 1857. And 100 years ago, in *Plessy vs. Ferguson* they decided that "separate but equal facilities" were O.K. In *The New York Times vs. Sullivan*, they rendered public figures virtually defenseless against defamation. It was a bad decision, and it should be revisited.

# # #

And then there's television. Television doesn't have the benefit of First Amendment protection to the extent that the print press has, and the problem with television isn't arrogance, it's commercialism.

It's commonplace these days to lump the print press, TV, and radio under a single banner called "the media". But the contrast between the print press and TV couldn't be greater. Newspapers began hundreds of years ago because of the strong urge to communicate built into the human species. The original penny press carried few or no advertisements. People put them out because they wanted to deliver a message from a particular point of view. Ben Franklin's "Poor Richard's Almanack" and the other penny newspapers of that time had much to do with the American Revolution and the creation of our country. Even today, new newspapers keep springing up all the time—including on the Internet, these days—because of our urge to communicate. The idea of selling advertising space in newspapers came along later.

But television had a different origin. From the beginning, the motive was to make money by selling advertising and to project on the screen whatever would hold the viewer's attention well enough to get them to watch the ads. Although TV news began as a public service, providing news has become just another way of selling ads.

And so, TV's first goal is to be entertaining, to attract viewers to watch, in order to sell those ads. And the ads keep getting more expensive every year. A thirty second spot during the Super Bowl sells for more than $2 million.

News shows on TV are consistently best sellers, even though there's precious little news in them. A typical 30-minute national newscast has no more than 20 minutes of actual news. In 20 measly minutes, Brokaw, Jennings, and Rather can't get out more than a few hundred actual words—although they do have the great advantage of *motion pictures* to help tell the story—while even a mid-size newspaper carries tens of thousands of words of actual news and commentary each day.

And so TV news is lacking in depth relative to what we can read in the print press. It doesn't have to be that way, of course. With 18 hours a day of programming and upwards of 50 cable channels already available, there's plenty of capacity to bring us all the information we could ever want, replete with the motion pictures. But because TV is basically an advertising medium and because the competition for those advertising revenues is so fierce, the incentive of the TV networks is entirely in the direction of *viewership*, not information transmission, education, or quality programming. The more people that watch a TV station, the higher the rates the station can charge their advertisers. The most closely watched report that any TV station manager monitors is the Nielsen ratings. How many people are watching? The manager's salary is based on those ratings, not to mention the profits of the station owners. That's the source of the old TV newsroom adage, "If it bleeds, it leads", meaning that the news director tries to put the bloodiest, most gripping story at the top of the newscast: Hook 'em early, and you won't lose 'em to some competing channel.

In the early days of radio, the push was for information dissemination. There *were* no ads. There are several excellent histories detailing the birth of radio, TV, and the Federal Communications Commission (FCC). Lawrence Grossman's 1995 book, "The Electronic Republic", is one of the best. As he points out, the airwaves have long been considered public property and their use was intended for the public good. But corporate advertisers recognized early on the power of radio, and then TV, to *sell us stuff*. The requirement of providing for the public good, which is written into the FCC's charter, was slowly whittled away and is now virtually forgotten. Still, each radio and TV station must renew its license regularly and a condition of that renewal is that they set aside at least some of their air time for public service. The time set aside and the content it provides have become laughable. Commercial TV is big business. In recent years, GE bought NBC, Disney-Capital

Cities bought ABC, and Westinghouse bought CBS. Actually, Westinghouse not only *bought* CBS, but Westinghouse even *became* CBS in name, the old light-bulb, electric-generator, and railroad-brake portion of the company having been sold off.

True, there's an occasional documentary, or other information-laden program out there, especially on PBS or C-SPAN. But the commercial channels have been so effective at luring the viewing audience their way with sensationalism and entertainment that relatively few people even watch the good documentaries that PBS produces. Even programs like PBS's "Frontline" can pull their punches, thanks to corporate funding pressures, and ABC once pulled an entire anti-tobacco show when threatened with a multi-billion dollar lawsuit by R.J. Reynolds.

Some years ago, Turner Broadcasting produced a show describing the destruction of our national forests due to overcutting and clearcutting practices. It was entitled "Rage Over Trees" and, while it provided some balance, it clearly leaned toward the conservationist/preservationist point of view. But at the last minute, first one sponsor pulled out, then another, each presumably pressured by the timber industry and their corporate friends to do so. By show time, *every* sponsor had withdrawn — Coors, Ford, All-State, Citicorp, and others — but Ted Turner, to his eternal credit, ran the show anyway, without sponsors and therefore without commercial interruption. It was a lesson in corporate power and their control over the media. A single, distinct message like that can have a chilling effect on the entire industry.

Another example of corporate control took place during the 1993-'94 debate over the Clinton healthcare plan. With all of its confusion, the Clinton plan was really a quite modest step forward in providing universal access to healthcare. It was far from the single-payer plan that most enlightened nations of the world enjoy. Still, it was attacked from the get-go by reactionaries of all stripes, but particularly by those who might have had something to lose: the health insurance industry. Their "Harry and Louise" ads, run nationwide to the tune of tens of millions of dollars, induced enough fear and uncertainty in the American public that the Clinton plan was defeated, without even enjoying a vote in Congress.

The lesson to be learned here is that TV has become *the* medium by which to reach people and to convince them of a certain point of view. But buying time on TV is also atrociously expensive, well beyond the means of the average citizen or medium-size public interest group, meaning that only major corporations or other well funded organizations like labor unions have the wherewithal to get on TV with their message.

And the message, to be effective, must be repeated enough times that the average viewer will see it multiple times. Let's face it: that's why we buy Ford Explorers, Viagra, AOL Internet services, Budweiser beer, Pepsi, and everything else we buy—we've seen their catchy ads on TV enough times that they have made an imprint. It's *repetition* that counts.

A legitimate question to ask is, what does it cost in pure advertising to change the way Americans think about something—*any*thing? Gun control, for example, or campaign finance reform. I don't know, but I'll bet there are people at Philip Morris, Procter and Gamble, and General Motors who do know.

When I first ran for the Senate in 1990, and observed how expensive TV ads were, I attempted to buy up *all* the ads in a typical 30-minute TV show and replace the show with 30 minutes of my message. It would cost a lot more than a single spot, of course, but at least I could actually *say* something to the voters, which is virtually impossible in a 30-second spot.

But I was unsuccessful. The stations won't even sell a 30-minute slot. Their explanation is that they contract with the producers of "Bay Watch," for example, for 26 episodes. If they sold a 30-minute slot during the period when "Bay Watch" was supposed to run, it would disrupt their contract. But the *real* reason, I believe, is that they don't want any politician interrupting their normal evening sequence of shows, especially in these days of the "remote." If a politician came on, it's too easy for the viewers to switch to another channel, and then they're lost for the remainder of the evening, and maybe more.

Still, in Ross Perot's '92 campaign, he bought several 30-minute and even 60-minute slots for his infomercials. I believe that he succeeded where others have failed because he promised to buy a great deal of time in 30-second spots, and because he had great name I.D., and his infomercials were interesting and held the viewer's attention.

But there's no guarantee. In '96, Perot's attempts to buy 30-minute slots were turned down, over his bitter protests. Apparently by the time of his second presidential campaign the networks felt he was old news, or discredited, and that he wouldn't hold those audiences.

But Perot's massive purchase of paid TV time also bought him a lot of free TV coverage. When Ralph Nader ran for president in '96, he bought *no* TV time and therefore received almost no free time, either. He received more free coverage during his 2000 presidential campaign, when he was buying 30-second spots.

Many of us thought that the answer to the super-commercialization of television was to be found in *public* TV, PBS, the Public Broadcasting Service. At its inception, public TV was a great idea, and with all of its limitations – especially monumental underfunding – the best shows on TV, for many of us, are to be found on PBS. But it, too, feels the pressure of the commercial channels and in its effort to compete PBS becomes more commercial all the time, as brought home in James Ledbetter's 1997 book, "Made Possible By..." "The News Hour with Jim Lehrer" is made possible by Archer Daniels Midland, among other sponsors. If ADM gets itself in a *real* scrape with the law – and it has already suffered some damaging scrapes – what are the chances we'll get the real skinny on "The News Hour"?

As Ledbetter points out, Japan spends $32 annually per capita on its public broadcasting TV system, England spends $39 and Canada spends $31. Here in the U.S., we spend a measly $1.09 and many in Congress want to cut that to zero! If we want unbiased, unfiltered information on the nation and the world, PBS is the place to find it, and we should be prepared to pay for it.

In the U.K. and in most other democracies, candidates for office can't even buy TV spots. Campaigns are much shorter and they are subsidized almost universally by the government (but *not* in the U.S., except for the presidential elections and a few places where voters have approved publicly funded elections). If we tried to limit political ads on TV in this country we'd run into the First Amendment and its freedom of speech clause. Television advertising in the U.S. is the most expensive in the world and, with the promised advent of the 500-channel future, it will become only more expensive, continually driving up the spiraling costs of election campaigns.

# # #

Television has further reduced the level of candor between elected officials or candidates for public office and the public. How many times have we witnessed a member of Congress, while being interviewed on television, give evasive answers or non-answers or "sound-bite" answers? It's not an accident. There are two reasons for it. First, television has become geared to sound-bites. Air time is now so precious and competition with the 49 other channels so severe that most stations *want* short answers, even if they have no content. PBS and C-SPAN do a vastly better job here than the major networks. Their stock-in-trade is in-depth discussion of issues.

A second reason for politician's waffling or evading is their fear of the next election campaign. I know; I was coached by my first campaign manager, Karen Olick, to *not* answer the interviewer's questions but to make my statement on the issue, to "stay on message." One simple slip of the tongue, one politically incorrect statement can be used by one's opponent in a potentially devastating 30-second spot that can put the politician in permanent retirement. So the tough questions — on drugs and crime, or abortion, or gun control, or stem-cell research, or even campaign finance reform — receive canned answers, carefully crafted in advance to not alienate people on either side of the issue. All we can hope for is tough interviewers who ask follow-up questions and insist on straight answers. The overall lack of candor of politicians has certainly fed the growing cynicism toward elected officials and our distrust of them. As positive models, we can hold up Arizona Senator John McCain and Minnesota Governor Jesse Ventura. Both are given to straight talk, in fact they take pride in it, and both have lived to tell about it.

# # #

Paul Taylor, a respected former reporter for The Washington Post, left the Post in 1995 to form a new group, first known as "The Free TV for Straight Talk Coalition" and now called "The Alliance for Better Campaigns." It is co-chaired by Jimmy Carter, Walter Cronkite, and Gerald Ford. Its purpose is to convince the TV networks to provide free TV time to qualified candidates for office, to allow them to reach their audience with their message. That one step alone would make a major, positive change in the corrupt election system we now live in by, first, eliminating the necessity to raise all that campaign money to buy the TV time and, second, giving the candidates enough time to actually *say* something to the voters, instead of simply flying the flag, mumbling some platitudes, and attacking the opponent.

The networks don't like Taylor's idea one bit—why give away all that time when they aren't forced to? Taylor's initial objective was to have the networks provide a mere five minutes for each of the presidential candidates. And he wanted to have the time blocked, so that all channels in each TV market carried the messages at the same time—to avoid channel surfing when the candidates came on the air. After months of wrangling, some of the networks agreed to provide the free time, but they wouldn't agree to block out the time: a partial victory. Taylor had a bit more success in the 2000 elections. One would hope that Taylor's idea could be broadened to provide blocked time for *real* candidate debates—real debates, wherein the candidates are free to ask one another the tough questions and insist on honest answers. Such debates should include, however, outside candidates like Ralph Nader who haven't bought into the present corrupt-money-in-politics scam, who can ask the other candidates where their campaign money has come from and who they're indebted to. If done right, Taylor's idea could be the start of a voter reconnect, one that is sorely needed in view of the record low voter turnout in recent elections.

We also need a restoration of the so-called Fairness Doctrine. The Fairness Doctrine was introduced by Congressional mandate in 1949. It required broadcasters to cover controversial issues within their community as well as nationally, and to do so by offering balancing views. We're brainwashed by the military-industrial complex into believing we need a $300 billion annual defense budget. Why shouldn't the millions of people who think half that much would still be plenty—people with no voice—be allowed to present a counter argument? The Fairness Doctrine was actually only a timid first step toward *true* democracy but, alas, Ronald Reagan threw it out in 1987 by executive order. Against heavy lobbying from the National Association of Broadcasters, several attempts to revive it since then have failed. Reagan vetoed the bill the first time it passed both houses of Congress, and President Bush (the elder) threatened to veto a similar bill in 1989 and it never got through the Senate. President George W. Bush could reinstitute the Fairness Doctrine with a stroke of his pen, by executive order (but don't hold your breath).

We've actually been making negative progress in allowing legitimate voices to be heard. In 2000, the FCC ruled that TV stations did not have to provide rebuttal time to opinions they, the stations, expressed. The

Harry Lonsdale

FCC's logic was that the requirement of rebuttal time was infringing on the *station's* right to free speech. From here, it again seems like more power in fewer hands.

# # #

Having run for statewide political office in Oregon, I had my share of tangles with the press, as this chapter illustrates. For me, the most difficult part of running for office — and one of the major reasons that more good people don't — was in having to deal with the press. Here are some of the conclusions I've come away with:

- Members of the press suffer from some of the same faults that all of the rest of us suffer from. They can be arrogant, unfair, biased, cowardly, profit-driven, egotistical, and more. Rarely, they can even be heroic. Having said all of that, I wouldn't trade our freedom of the press for any sort of controlled or government-run system. Nor do I advocate censorship. On the contrary, press exposés undoubtedly strengthen our democracy. I do think, however, that delving into the private lives of public figures has gone too far. It has led to a great deal of distrust between the press and elected officials.

- The simple act of having editorial writers sign their editorials would bring a great measure of civility to the discourse between the print press and politicians. I believe that it would enhance our trust in both the press *and* in politicians.

- The Supreme Court decision in *The New York Times vs. Sullivan* went too far, and it should be revisited by the courts. Being at the mercy of newspaper editors with their overly broad protections can leave even honest elected officials the subject of unwarranted scorn and ridicule. No wonder they rate so low in national opinion polls.

- But I reserve my harshest criticism for television. It seems that TV has now become so thoroughly commercialized that there's no redeeming it in this country.

While we may never succeed in getting politicians to talk straight to us, we could afford them with free TV time during election season, if the time were used not for self-serving chest-thumping or demagoguery but for concise presentation of their positions on issues and for debating their opponents. Driving distrust and cynicism out of our political discourse won't be easy; it's firmly established. But we can start, by using TV — our public airwaves, after all — to create a national dialogue between the governed and the governors. Imagine TV being used to inform us of where our tax money went and then asking us — We The People — to decide if that was what we wanted. We need the Federal Communications Commission to enforce that provision in law that requires television stations to provide for public service in exchange for their free licenses. Like Jefferson, I trust the people to make the right decisions concerning their personal interests, if they are fairly and fully informed.

Finally, and most importantly, we need a truly public TV network, a network so well endowed, so uncompromised, and so appealing that people will actually watch it. The power of TV is enormous, surely comparable at this point to the power of the print press. That power is being largely wasted, converting us into the world's greatest consumer society. It could, instead, convert us into the best informed, most democratic society the world has ever known.

CHAPTER 7.

CAMPAIGN FINANCE REFORM AND DEMOCRACY

Money and politics have been intertwined since the beginnings of our republic. No doubt the fusion dates back to the Greek and Roman "democracies," and even before. There is scant documentation of it in the early histories of the United States, but we can have no doubt that vote-buying and vote-swapping were commonplace. How else to explain that slavery was institutionalized in our Constitution (without the word "slave" ever being mentioned)?

The biggest land-giveaway in U.S. history – millions of acres given to the railroads in the 1860s to build the transcontinental railroad – was made possible by gifts of railroad company stock to members of Congress. The giveaway also made railroad barons Leland Stanford, Mark Hopkins, the Crocker brothers, and their heirs filthy rich. The "robber barons" – in steel, oil, banking, and elsewhere – continued to have enormous influence on our elected officials throughout the late 19th and early 20th Centuries. Teddy Roosevelt and his "trust busters" began reforms almost a century ago, and Americans have been pushing for enhanced reforms ever since.

But for every reform, it seems, there's a loophole. A litany of the current loopholes that should shame us all are portrayed in the hilarious 1990s film, "The Distinguished Gentleman," available at your favorite video store: phony foundations, speaking fees, Super Bowl tickets, free flights on corporate jets, scholarships for the children of Congressmembers, free use of condos in Vail, and, of course, campaign contributions.

What is outrageous about all of these influence-buying schemes is that all of them are perfect *legal*. And they're only legal, of course, because Congress has declared them legal. They're clearly unethical or simply downright corrupt. The big campaign contributions are nothing more than legalized bribes. Campaign contributions certainly aren't the only reason that politicians vote the way they do. But most of us would agree that contributions shouldn't have *any* impact on how they vote.

Growing national concern over the influence of money in politics led to the Federal Election Campaign Act of 1974, which established the Federal Election Commission (FEC), put limits on federal campaign contributions and expenditures (the latter later repealed), allowed the establishment of political action committees (PACs) and, to hear Congress tell it, "cleaned up the system". But it didn't. The system is probably no more corrupt today than it was 100 years ago; in fact, it's almost certainly *less* corrupt. It's still corrupt, but now it's out in the open. We can thank the media and the good-government organizations cited later in this chapter for that.

The godfather of campaign finance reform would have to be the late Philip M. Stern, whose two books, "The Best Congress Money Can Buy" (1988) and "*Still* the Best Congress Money Can Buy" (1992), are still the classics in the field. In the front material to the second book, Stern gives us an imaginary scenario first suggested by former Democratic Senator Bill Proxmire of Wisconsin. It goes something like this:

> It's the seventh and deciding game of the World Series, at Yankee Stadium. Before the opening pitch, the pitcher walks up to home plate, peels off one hundred $100 bills and hands them to the umpire. The ump pockets the money, the pitcher returns to the mound, and the ump shouts, "play ball." The fans, initially stunned into silence, erupt in protest. How can the umpire possibly call a fair game with $10,000 of the pitcher's money stuffed in his pocket?
>
> Later, after the game is postponed because all the fans have left the stadium—after throwing everything they can lay their hands on at the umpire—the ump denies that his judgement would have been in any way influenced by the money.

Bill Proxmire served with distinction in the U.S. Senate for 31 years. If anyone should know how the system works, it is he. In his last election campaign, he told me one day as we spoke near his office in the Library of Congress, he spent only about $600, almost all of it for postage to return campaign contributions!

In an article in the Columbia Law Review of May 1994, Fred Wertheimer and Susan Weiss Manes reproduce this quotation, dealing with a Congressman's loyalties:

"What happens is a gradual shifting of a man's loyalties from the community to those who have been doing him favors. His final decisions are, therefore, made in response to his private friendships and loyalties, rather than to the public good. Throughout this whole process, the official will claim — and may indeed believe — that there is no causal connection between the favors he has received and the decisions which he makes. He will assert that the favors were given and received on the basis of pure friendship unsullied by worldly considerations. He will claim that the decisions, on the other hand, will have been made on the basis of the justice and equity of the particular case. The two series of acts will be as separate as the east is from the west. Moreover, the whole process may be so subtle as not to be detected by the official himself."

That quotation was taken, not from a current piece in The Nation, but rather from an article by former Illinois Senator Paul Douglas entitled "Ethics in Government" that he wrote in 1952. That's long before the advent of modern, super-expensive, TV-driven congressional and presidential election campaigns.

My wife has spent most of her adult life working in TV news. A few years back, she came up with the following idea. You know those race-car drivers and their race cars, where every square inch, it seems, is used to display an ad for anything from Pennzoil to Budweiser? Well, she suggests that our members of Congress, on the floor of the House and Senate and on C-SPAN, should display the logos for all the corporations they're *really* representing: the Met Life "Snoopy", the McDonald's golden arches, the Marlboro Man, the Nike "Swoosh", and all the rest — on their lapels, shirt collars, breast pockets, even on little caps they could be provided. It wouldn't be pretty, but it would at least be honest. But my wife isn't alone in making that suggestion; she may not even be first. I've found it done up nicely in Jim Hightower's hilarious but thought-provoking book, "There's Nothing in the Middle of the Road But Yellow Stripes and Dead Armadillos."

On some of the walls of the Air Force Academy in Colorado Springs is the Academy honor code. It's simple but powerful: "We will not lie, cheat, or steal, nor tolerate among us anyone who does." So simple. So powerful. At the opening of the U.S. House and Senate chambers each day, the members pledge allegiance to the flag and then listen to a short prayer. Too bad they don't recite the AFA honor code every day, instead. And then, live by it.

Let's see if we can't reduce this whole ugly mess to a simple chart. In the chart below, I represent all of those who contribute money to candidates, usually incumbents, running for office and who *want* something afterwards—as special interests.

Politicians, Money, and Votes

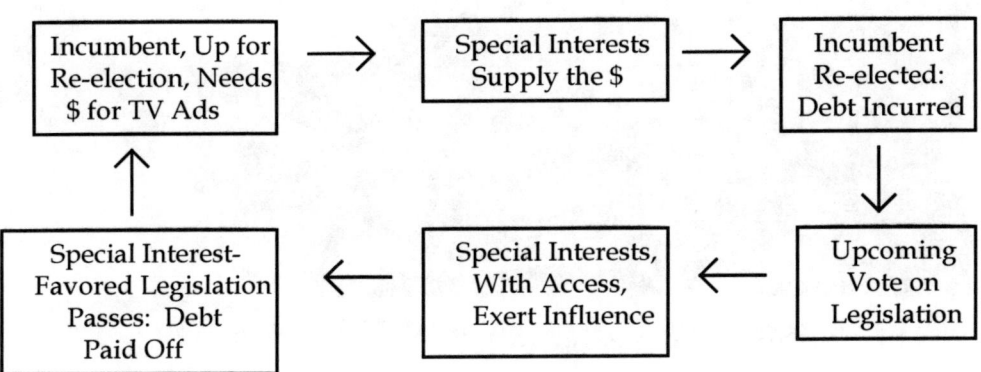

When I say that the special interests "want something," I imply that the thing they want is *not* cleaner government, or a more representative democracy: they want votes on specific pieces of legislation—which they, the special interest lobbyists, may even help to write—legislation that will somehow advance their cause, which usually translates into "make them more money." In some cases, what they want is the *absence* of legislation; that is, they want an unfavorable bill killed and not even discussed on the floor of the House or Senate.

Some special interests create PACs with which to funnel their money into campaigns. Large corporations can simply bundle $1000 contributions from a few dozen corporate executives, and their spouses (and their kids, if they're really desperate), and make a major contribution to the incumbent, one that will incur that debt. Some bundlers of money, like EMILYs list, use their money for purposes that I

Rob Rogers
Pittsburgh Post-Gazette
United Media Group

Rob Rogers reprinted by permission of United Feature Syndicate, Inc.

happen to agree with: EMILYs list works to elect more women to Congress. And not all influence is bought through direct contributions to candidates. Increasingly in recent years, the really big contributions come as "soft money," which is money contributed to political parties. Corporations or individuals can legally contribute unlimited amounts of soft money, and contributions of $100,000 and more have become commonplace.

A key word in the above chart is "access." Many members of Congress claim that all they're offering their cash constituents is access. But access shouldn't be for sale.

*Running
Politics, Power, and the Press*

Jack Ohman, The Oregonian. Reprinted with permission.

I use the word "incumbent" on purpose. Almost all incumbents who run for re-election win and when the incumbent dies or retires or resigns, the scramble is on, as the challengers for the open seat court the special interests to show that they, too, can be bought.

Let's take a closer look at that Politicians, Money, and Votes chart.

INCUMBENT, UP FOR RE-ELECTION, NEEDS $ FOR TV ADS

Incumbents are up every two years in the U.S. House, every six years in the U.S. Senate. Terms of office for state legislatures vary from state to state. "Needs $"? Campaigns have become almost exclusively media wars. TV spots cost a *lot* of money. One 30-second spot, in Portland, Oregon, on *one* station, in prime time can cost $15,000!

Harry Lonsdale

SPECIAL INTERESTS SUPPLY THE $

The Center for Responsive Politics and Common Cause, both in Washington, D.C., have extensive records of contributions from corporations, unions, and wealthy individuals.

INCUMBENT RE-ELECTED: DEBT INCURRED

With all the anger directed at Congress, incumbents *do* get re-elected regularly. Strom Thurmond turned 99 in 2001, and he's been in the Senate since 1955, both as a Democrat and as a Republican.

As for "DEBT INCURRED", that's harder to prove, of course. If there were no debt, why would the special interests give the money? For fifteen years, I was the president and CEO of a small high tech company in Bend, Oregon. Especially in our early years of poverty, I watched every significant expenditure like a hawk. When we spent money, we were almost always buying something: supplies, paying the rent, paying salaries, whatever. We *never* threw money away. And special interests and wealthy individuals don't either. In the rare event that the elected official turns against the money source, the money is cut off, and the money source looks for someone new in the next election cycle, even if that turns out to be the *opponent* of the person they have already invested in in the past.

UPCOMING VOTE ON LEGISLATION

There are thousands of votes every session, most of them having some economic impact on someone, even if it's only us taxpayers.

SPECIAL INTERESTS, WITH ACCESS, EXERT INFLUENCE

It's rarely a straight-up *quid pro quo*: "Here's the money, we want your vote." It's usually subtle, seductive, maybe a wink and a nod, frequently not even that. The politician knows how he or she is expected to vote by the money source that wrote the check. And he or she knows that the money source keeps score.

SPECIAL INTEREST-FAVORED LEGISLATION PASSES: DEBT PAID OFF

Fortunately for us, former U.S. Senator Bob Packwood kept a detailed diary for years. In the mid-'90s, the Senate Select Committee on Ethics held private hearings to consider Packwood's expulsion from the Senate for making unwelcome sexual advances toward several women and other transgressions. In the course of those hearings, his diary came into question. Transcripts of the diary, possibly altered, and audiotapes, were reviewed by the Committee, and parts thereof are included in the revealing book, *The Packwood Report* (Times Books, 1995). Here's one little excerpt from the book. Bill Furman is president of Greenbrier Companies of Lake Oswego, Oregon and a major contributor to Packwood's Senate campaigns. Among other things, Greenbrier makes and leases railroad cars. In 1990, Furman was quoted as saying, "Bob, there's no *quid pro quo*. You've done so much for my company and so much for this state and I just want to do anything I can to make your continued existence in politics possible".

There's a lot more blockbuster material in *The Packwood Report*, too much to try to summarize here. Packwood subtly but publicly threatened to blow the Senate's collective cover on the matter of trading campaign contributions for votes if they didn't let him off. Not surprisingly, the Ethics Committee rejected holding public hearings but did agree to release all the evidence in the case. And then they voted unanimously to recommend Packwood's expulsion from the Senate. Instead, he resigned.

In the Politicians, Money, and Votes chart, one might ask, "Where's the citizens' input?" Who represents you and me in that loop? The answer is no one, unless you're in the loop with a major campaign contribution. But less than 0.1% of Americans *are* in that loop.

We aren't totally silenced, of course. You're still free to write a letter to your Congressperson or state legislator, or even pay a visit, or phone or fax or e-mail your input. Or, better yet, attend one of those town hall meetings that your elected representative probably holds in the district occasionally. And I'm sure the elected official, or her/his aide, will respond to your request with some form letter, maybe even a *non*-form letter. In the unlikely event that your point of view is shared by enough people *who also make their viewpoint known to the elected official*, you might

Harry Lonsdale

" I THOUGHT HE WAS A MEMBER OF A SPECIAL INTEREST GROUP... BUT I FOUND OUT HE'S ONLY A VOTER ! "

Wayne Stayskal, The Tampa Tribune. Reprinted with permission.

even prevail without ever sending in a campaign contribution. But, chances are, your single voice is totally drowned out by the special interests, their money, and their lobbyists.

Jeff Mapes, a first rate reporter for The Oregonian, questioned me more than once when I was running for office about the difference, if any, between PAC money and non-PAC money. In the case of PACs, you *know* they want something when the election is over. Private, individual contributions, on the other hand, at least have the potential of being made for the public good. And the small contributions almost certainly are made that way. With the $1000 contributions there's no assurance. I was never elected, and so I can't address the question, "did any of my contributors expect something after the election?" But when I received a $1000 contribution from some total stranger in Alaska, for example, I had reason to wonder.

The state of Oregon publishes, after each election cycle, a list of all of the cash contributions over $100 to people running for statewide office (governor, secretary of state, etc.) and all contributions over $50 to people running for the legislature. It's called the Contributions and Expenditures Report, available inexpensively from the secretary of state's office. Most states produce similar reports. The Federal Election Commission and public interest groups in Washington, D.C., keep track of all such contributions to people running for federal office: the Congress and the president and vice president. An examination of those reports shows that some individuals and special interest groups contribute to *opposing* candidates ... even though they know that their names will ultimately be printed in a report somewhere for all to see. That's buying access. They don't care who wins; they just want access to the winner.

In the campaign finance reform debate, some people argue for taking off all limits on contributions and just providing for full disclosure of the contributions. But that simply wouldn't work. Merely disclosing something doesn't automatically put it in front of the voters' eyes, let alone enter it into their brains; for that, we need the TV stations and newspapers to run the material repeatedly, like those TV spots are run; but that doesn't happen.

Several hard-working public interest groups have tried to tie campaign contributions to votes on legislation. It's virtually impossible. First, because there are so few straight up or down votes on bills in Congress. What with amendments and different versions of a bill on a particular issue, Congresspersons can legitimately claim that they voted *for*—and, in a different gathering, *against*—seemingly identical legislation. But, more importantly, we'll never know what goes on in their brains as they vote. What factors are they weighing? Some revealing books have been written by Congressmembers about this subject, all, fittingly, after they have left office or at least after they have announced that they won't seek re-election. A partial list of such books, along with others dealing with politics, the press, and campaign finance, all fascinating reading, can be found in the Bibliography.

Public interest groups have shown a solid correlation between contributions from the sugar lobby and how members of Congress vote on the sugar subsidy every time it comes up for a vote. But even a perfect correlation doesn't prove *intent*. And how many people really care that they pay an extra nickel a pound for sugar?

Harry Lonsdale

Toles ©2001 The Buffalo News. Reprinted with permission of Universal Press Syndicate. All rights reserved.

Perhaps the closest we've come so far to a confession about the influence of money in politics was a remark made several years ago by Louisiana Senator John Breaux who, when asked if his vote was for sale, jokingly replied, "No, but it's for rent."

# # #

It's legitimate to ask, why all this fuss about money in politics? Why should we care? How does all of that supposed vote-buying affect me? I've listed below a handful of the things that our state and federal governments should be doing — or, in some cases, *not* doing. I believe that if you put it to a vote of the American people today—*without propaganda from either side skewing the result*—they would vote in the majority for each position advocated here.

1. Guaranteed Healthcare for Every Citizen, Throughout Life.

Every industrialized nation in the world has it, except our own. Some countries have had a system of national healthcare in place for two generations, while we're still debating the idea. Talk to any Canadian and you'll find that he or she loves their single-payer healthcare system, in spite of the horror stories you've heard in the U.S. about the Canadian system. And the evidence points to the fact that here in the U.S. we pay for healthcare for every citizen whether we know it or not, and whether we want to or not. People without health insurance postpone visits to the doctor when they're sick because they can't afford to pay for them. Many of them eventually wind up in the emergency room, for the most expensive kind of healthcare there is. And so we, those of us who buy medical insurance, or our employers who buy it for us, pay the bill for the uninsured through higher premiums.

The Clintons tried to institute a national healthcare plan early in President Clinton's first term. The president held up a plastic card, during a nationally televised event, indicating that every American would be issued such an identifying card to use for any visit to a doctor's office, medical emergency, or any other healthcare need. The polls in those days showed that a large majority of Americans favored national healthcare, including the idea of a single-payer system.

Then the special interests on this issue took the gloves off. The special interests in this case constitute all of those involved in the healthcare industry who benefit from the status quo: doctors, nurses, hospitals, small business groups, and the pharmaceutical companies. At the top of the list is the health insurance industry. For the most part, their public approach was subtle—they introduced doubt: We'd all suffer long waiting lines, no personal physicians, lower quality care, socialized medicine, the end of pharmaceutical research that brings us new medicines, and so on. They bombarded us with $40 million of TV ads. Meanwhile, they privately lobbied Congress heavily.

Along the way, the question arose, "Should healthcare be a *right*, enjoyed by every citizen?" There's no question that we'd have to pay for it (if not us, *who*?) and, in that sense, it's not a right. But small business owners became opponents of a universal healthcare plan when it became clear that one option would be to have *them* provide coverage for all of their employees. One answer to that problem might be to let the taxpayers pay for national healthcare through the income tax and other taxes, as Canadians do; free the employers from providing healthcare for their employees; and have the employers give their employees a raise, representing the employer's saving and the employee's new burden. It would represent a major shift in how things are done, to be sure, but it's certainly doable.

In the end, even normally fair-minded Americans opposed national healthcare—at least the Clintons' version thereof—thanks to massive propagandizing and heavy-duty lobbying. The Clinton plan never even came up for a vote in Congress.

The opponents of national healthcare would have us overlook the fact that everyone over 65 in our country—and everyone below the poverty line—already has national healthcare: we call it Medicare and Medicaid. More than 60 million of us, almost a quarter of the population, already *have* national healthcare (including all members of Congress, of course.). In his lame-duck years, President Clinton proposed that we extend Medicare down to the near-retirees, those aged 62-65, as a way of incrementally extending Medicare. And 2000 presidential candidate Al Gore proposed guaranteeing healthcare to all children. None of that has happened yet.

Thus, something that polls showed that 70% or more of Americans favored five or ten years ago hasn't yet come to pass thanks to the powerful influence of money in politics. Until some insider writes a book, we may never know the extent of the lobbying pressure and the outright threats that went into defeating the Clinton healthcare plan.

Even after the Clinton healthcare plan went down, Americans still wanted universal coverage. A 1994 nationwide poll showed that 79% of us said that it was "very important" that every American receive health insurance coverage. Why don't we have it?!

2. End the Military-Industrial Complex

The U.S. now spends more than 40% of the world's total expenditures on arms. Far and away, we are the world's largest arms exporter. When

American troops on some peacekeeping mission are shot at or have missiles sent their way, chances are that those armaments were "Made in the U.S.A." The military budget is more than $300 billion a year, or more than $1000 for every American citizen. Stories of waste, fraud, kickbacks, and unnecessary and unworkable weapon systems fill the press. Most recently, it's the so-called missile shield. Even if it can be made to work, it wouldn't defend us from a nuclear attack delivered by boat, truck, or airplane.

Eisenhower warned us about it in a speech he delivered early in his presidency: "Every gun that is made, every warship launched, every rocket fired signifies, in the final sense, a theft from those who hunger and are not fed, those who are cold and are not clothed." In his farewell address to the nation, he coined the term "military-industrial complex." This, from a Republican president, who led the allied forces in Europe in W.W.II. Almost half a century later, it's still going on.

The most powerful lobby back in Washington, D.C., is the U.S. military-industrial lobby. Thanks to the investigative press, we know who they are, and we know how they operate: we're just powerless to stop them. They're organized, and they have election-campaign money to shower on their friends and on the enemies of their enemies. All we have is talk, and a majority opinion. In the final analysis, isn't the solution to the worldwide arms chase a broad-based, credible U.N. peacekeeping force, with the U.S. as a major participant? Why hasn't that surfaced as a topic for national debate?

3. Effective Gun Control

Some of my best friends are gun owners. But like most Americans, I'm appalled by all the killings, both intentional and accidental, that occur in our country. The National Rifle Association claims a national membership of close to three million people, a figure that's down somewhat since they called the federal agents "jack-booted thugs" after the Waco debacle, resulting in ex-President George Bush and many others quitting the NRA in disgust. So, if three million people belong, that means that about 280 million or 99% of us *don't* belong. We're the overwhelming majority and we want effective gun control. They are a tiny minority, and they prevent it.

They succeed because they're organized; they raise money; they support their friends in Congress; and they can sometimes defeat their enemies. The late Mike Synar, former member of Congress from Oklahoma and one of the most outspoken opponents of guns, as well as one of the strongest supporters of campaign finance reform, was targeted by the NRA for several election cycles. They supplied campaign funds to his opponents. And he was ultimately defeated, in the 1994 Democratic primary election.

More people die from gunshot wounds in America in one day than die from the same cause in the U.K. or in Japan in an entire year! There are more than 200 million guns in the hands of private citizens in our country. This is the only industrialized country in the world where any non-felon can buy pretty much the gun of her or his choice. The latest craze is a 50-calibre, Barrett armor-piercing, semi-automatic weapon. In some states even felons can buy all the guns they want to, at gun swap meets. My gun-owning friends would willingly put their rifles and shotguns into storage, and have them registered in order to reduce gun violence. But the "gun nuts" I know think that anyone should be able to own any gun, including machine guns. Their proposal for reducing gun violence is to arm *everyone*.

With all their clout, what has the NRA done to try to keep guns out of the hands of criminals? Sadly, as long as money wins elections, we're going to lose this one, too.

4. Tobacco Regulated as a Drug

Cigarettes killed my father, and a lot of other fathers—and mothers. 400,000 Americans die each year, according to Surgeon Generals' reports, from smoking-related causes. That's more than 1000 Americans every day—more than die from AIDS, alcohol, car accidents, murders, suicides, drugs, and fire—*combined*. Billboards around the country proclaim, "500,000,000 people, now living, will die from tobacco." In his classic, Pulitzer-prize winning book, "Ashes to Ashes", author Richard Kluger points out that not only the U.S. Congress but every one of the 50 state legislatures have been bought off by the tobacco industry.

The tobacco industry suffered its first significant defeat in the late '90s. Lawsuits brought by sufferers of tobacco-induced diseases, or their heirs, began to go against the industry, which finally agreed to seek a

Congressional solution. In exchange for a proposed $300 billion-plus payment to the states for their unrecovered medical costs under Medicare, the industry sought eternal immunity from all lawsuits. Not even their friends in Congress and the state legislatures could bring that one off, however. The settlement finally reached calls for payment of $206 billion, paid out over 25 years, to the 46 states that brought suit. To the industry, it meant raising the price of tobacco products substantially, which their addicted customers continue to pay. The industry got no immunity, and lawsuits continue to go against them while they continue to search for new ways to addict teenagers, and to increase their product sales overseas. Smokers continue to die.

The only reasonable solution appears to be to regulate tobacco as a drug, which it clearly is. David Kessler, former head of the Food and Drug Administration, fought for tobacco regulation for years, unsuccessfully. (See his book, "A Question of Intent," Public Affairs, New York, 2001.) While weakened, the industry continues to wield enormous lobbying clout.

5. Save the Ancient Forests

Anyone who has seen some of the millions of acres of clearcuts on our federal lands, either on foot or from the window of an airplane, would say, "Stop! This is insanity."

But in Oregon the fix is in, as far as timber is concerned. It's just quietly understood that you don't get elected to any significant position if you take an anti-timber (read "pro-forest") stance. What's downright discouraging is how cheaply the fix has been bought, compared with the profits at stake. The timber barons, their companies, and their PACs don't even have to write really big checks to elected and to-be-elected officials. They're part of a statewide network of executives, as I learned when I served for a time on the Oregon Business Council, that are the unofficial kingmakers of the state. It's akin to the oil and gas network in Oklahoma, Texas, and Louisiana; or the mining industry in Colorado and Montana; or the insurance industry in Connecticut.

These timber barons have got things so wired that even the forest-lovers in many Oregon counties are hooked. That came about when Congress passed legislation dedicating a percentage of the timber receipts from each national forest to the counties that lie within or adjacent to that national forest. Thus, residents in many of Oregon's timber towns pay very little in property taxes because much of their road and school budgets are paid for out of the timber receipts. It was a great ploy for locking in local support for overcutting our national forests.

The trees standing in the national forests in Oregon alone are worth a conservative $100 billion—when reduced to timber. With their tidy profits, it's no wonder that the timber industry coughs up a few bucks to see that "right-thinking people" get elected and re-elected. Here, again, we lose until we change campaign finance laws. And the losers are all of us, along with our grandkids and future generations.

6. End Corporate Welfare

How bad is it? I suppose we'll never know with any accuracy, but in their booklet, "Take the Rich off Welfare," Mark Zepezauer and Arthur Naiman have put together some interesting examples of corporate welfare and the costs thereof to us taxpayers. It's well known out here in the West that ranching, logging, and mining have gotten and continue to get regular, massive tax breaks, or other forms of government largesse. Ranchers run their cattle and sheep all over leased government land for a fraction of what it would cost them to lease equivalent private land. Worse still, after they've run their cattle on our public land for a decade or so, they begin to think of it as *their* land. For years the timber companies ripped us off —legally, of course; remember, their friends in Congress make the laws—by having the U.S. Forest Service build the roads into the forests, at taxpayer expense, so that their log trucks can get in to "harvest" our trees.

The mining rip-off is also sensational. Any company, domestic or foreign, can, if they discover minerals on public land, extract the minerals, patent their claim, and then buy the land for $2.50 per acre. There is no other land for sale in our country for anything like that exceedingly low price.

But corporate welfare is found in hundreds of places, as David Korten describes in his important book, "When Corporations Rule the World". From the deductibility of interest and advertising expenses, to minuscule corporate income taxes (they now represent only 6% of total income taxes paid in the U.S., down from 20% of total income taxes in the '60s), to legally raiding corporate pension funds, to tax incentives to the pharmaceutical companies that manufacture their drugs in Puerto Rico, to subsidizing the overseas advertising by McDonald's and other companies, to the NAFTA and GATT trade agreements (which Americans opposed, according to the polls, but we got them anyway), the list goes on as long as the Congressional Record.

Most of it we never even hear about, in spite of the investigative press. The inquiring reporters are drowned out by the public relations flacks hired by the corporations, and by their all-time-record level of tax-deductible advertising.

Today, even the Republicans in Congress are talking about ending corporate welfare, consistent with their mantra about smaller government and lower taxes. And, indeed, some farm subsidies that have been in existence for a century have reportedly been cut or eliminated. Still, I'm betting on the corporations, at least until we fix campaign finance laws.

7. Truly Progressive Taxes

The U.S. probably has the lowest income tax rate in the industrialized world, and yet we probably complain about our taxes more than anyone. Most of the other advanced countries raise a good deal of their revenues through sin taxes—on booze and tobacco—or through gasoline or excise taxes. In Canada, a decent bottle of booze costs $40 and a pack of cigarettes goes for close to $6. Those are expressed in Canadian dollars, but, even though the Canadian dollar is only worth about 70¢ in the U.S., they pay much more in sin taxes than we do. And a gallon of gasoline in Western Europe, Japan, and most of the industrialized world goes for $3.50 - $5.00 U.S., two to three times what we pay, the difference being the tax.

But sin taxes, excise taxes, and all consumption taxes are regressive. That is, working people spend a higher percentage of their income on consumables than do the wealthy. We've maintained the notion in the U.S. for generations that taxes should be progressive, based on the ability to pay.

Still, the top income tax rate in the U.S. is less than 40%—and headed lower, now that the budget is better balanced—which is lower than almost anywhere else in the advanced world. When Michael Eisner, head of Disney, makes $200+ million in salary and bonuses in a single year, as he did recently, he gets to pocket at least 60% of that money. Some people would say he's entitled to it. But it does fuel the class warfare that the Republicans complain about. A good way to stop it would be to raise the tax rate on super-incomes.

During W.W.II the maximum income tax rate in our country was a whopping 90%. And no one quit their high paying job because of it. In Oregon, one hits the maximum state income tax rate at about the *poverty* level. Everyone above the poverty level pays at the same flat rate. That's regressive.

I believe that most Americans advocate progressive taxes simply for economic fairness. And taxes should be more progressive on corporations, too — even though taxes are just a cost of doing business to corporations, and they will just pass the increased taxes on to their customers. So be it. But big, profitable corporations should be in substantially higher tax brackets than start-ups or small businesses. It's that fairness thing again.

But we won't get fairer, more progressive income taxes in our country until we get the Big Money out of politics.

8. End State-Sanctioned Gambling

It wasn't long ago that when you thought about legalized gambling you thought of Monte Carlo or Las Vegas. Then came Atlantic City. In recent years, state legislatures all across the country, caught in the public's anti-tax mood but with increasing demands for services, turned to gambling as a new source of "painless" income. First it was the lotteries, then the mega-lotteries. In Oregon the various legalized gambling activities take in more than 6% of our state's annual budget.

And it isn't painless to those who partake, who tend to be blue-collar workers who can least afford the financial drain. "Gamblers Anonymous" groups have sprung up all over the country, and there's already the occasional suicide by someone who's deeply in gambling debt, with no apparent way out. The promoters, of course, don't even call it "gambling," preferring the euphemism "gaming", to appeal to our propriety.

In states with significant native-American populations, gambling has become the principal source of income and jobs on many of the reservations. In 1998, there was an initiative on the California ballot that opened up wholesale gambling on Indian reservations. More than $90 million, at that time a national record, was spent on that initiative: about $60+ million by the California tribes, who were in favor, and $20+ million by the Las Vegas gambling groups who were opposed because they didn't want to lose any of their California customers. Not a dime was spent by anti-gambling folks. The measure passed easily.

The majority of us oppose it. But, as in the other cases cited above, we're complacent and unorganized, while the promoters keep the state legislatures happy with revenues and campaign contributions. What chance do we have?

9. End Poverty

The continuing argument over immigration quotas, the minimum wage, and acceptable inflation and unemployment rates could easily be confused with a concerted corporate move to hold down wages. Twenty percent of our fellow citizens now live below the official poverty level, with little hope of ever rising above it.

Poverty is so eminently fixable in a wealthy country like ours that one can conclude that it is corporate America that wants a vast and sustained pool of ultra-cheap labor to choose from. They, and their friends in Congress, continue to maintain the minimum wage below the poverty level for a typical family. Significantly, the states and even some municipalities like Corvallis, Oregon, have raised the minimum wage ... by the voters' initiative, in most cases, of course.

10. True Public TV

Commercial television is a big business, and it's getting bigger every year. If we need any other reinforcement for that conclusion, recall that the networks are now owned by corporate giants, GE (NBC), Disney (ABC), Westinghouse (CBS), and News Corp. (FOX). More advertising dollars are spent in the U.S. on TV than in newspapers, magazines, billboards, radio, or any other advertising vehicle.

As we have already noted, in the early days of commercial radio, and again 30 years later when TV took off, the granting of a virtually free broadcasting license by the government carried with it an obligation on the part of the licensee to set aside a portion of the broadcast day for public service. The argument ran that "the airwaves belong to all of us," so licenses should be free as long as public service was rendered. But as time went on, public service time diminished, until now there is virtually none.

What we lose every day by not having true, fully funded public TV is incalculable. Think of what *could* be brought into our homes every day. In addition to the entire world of knowledge, there's the opportunity for unbiased news as well as a diversity of viewpoints, which we're not now getting. Surely there is no better vehicle for educating all of us about the great democratic experiment called America than public television.

In 1996 we had a golden opportunity, which may never come again, to fully fund public TV forever by including in the massive Telecommunications Act a stipulation that a licensing fee, to be used for public TV, would be required of all broadcasters in exchange for the goodies they received free, with that act: more frequencies, the ability to own even more stations in a given market than they were already allowed, and more. But the moment passed. The industry lobbyists won again.

# # #

DEMOCRACY

These ten issues remain unresolved today largely because of the influence of Big Money in politics. But as big as any one of these issues is, and as big as they all are collectively, there's still something bigger at stake. It's what we call our democracy. Our democracy isn't healthy. Less than half of eligible voters vote, the lowest rate in any democracy in the world; and both major political parties are losing membership to people who prefer Independent or third-party status. Cynicism and distrust of government are rampant. New phrases tell the story: the Lincoln bedroom, the Buddhist temple, "no controlling legal authority." People don't vote because they feel that their vote doesn't make any difference—someone else is calling the shots.

*Running
Politics, Power, and the Press*

The last great spokesperson for the average American—at least the last who had any real influence on our lives—was Franklin Delano Roosevelt. In her extraordinary book of the W.W.II years of Franklin and Eleanor Roosevelt, "No Ordinary Time", Doris Kearns Goodwin paraphrases part of FDR's 1941 State of the Union address: "As the country committed itself to national defense ... it must never forget the goals for which it was fighting: equality of opportunity, jobs for those who could work, security for the needy, the ending of special privilege for the few, the preservation of civil liberties for all." And in his 1944 State of the Union address, just months before his death, he laid out his vision for America even more clearly. Again, according to Goodwin, Roosevelt argued that "a second Bill of Rights was needed to provide a new basis of security and prosperity for every American, regardless of race, color, or creed. That economic Bill of Rights must include: the right to a useful and remunerative job; to earnings sufficient for adequate food and clothing and recreation; to decent housing; to adequate medical care; to protection from the economic fears of old age and unemployment; to a good education."

In his humorous, enlightening, and provocative book, "There's Nothing In the Middle of the Road But Yellow Stripes and Dead Armadillos", Jim Hightower shrinks FDR's message down to three goals that we should continually strive for in our society: social justice, economic fairness, and equal opportunity.

Back in 1787, James Madison warned us about factions in his Federalist No. 10. In today's lexicon, "factions" equal special interests. Factions are everywhere, and they run the show: AARP, AFL-CIO, the NRA, and far and away the most important, corporate America or, more accurately, the transnational corporations. Those groups, and dozens more like them, supply the bulk of the hard and soft money that determine election outcomes in our country.

And that leads us to a serious weakness in our republican form of government. Thus, if the health insurance industry, for example, wants to survive, by defeating single-payer health coverage in our country, they don't have to convince all 280 million of us, or even half of us. All they really have to convince is half of the 435 members of the House of Representatives and half of the 100 U.S. Senators. In reality, all they need is a few key members of each body, chairs of committees and subcommittees; plus a few ranking members; and a few dozen other members of Congress who agree with them or to whom healthcare is not a major concern (or who are willing to trade their vote away for something that is more important to them). They can achieve those goals by direct lobbying, PAC contributions, and some letters from constituents back home, which may be either real or arranged by the industry itself.

When the power to affect all of our lives rests in only a few hands, it makes it relatively easy for the special interests to achieve their goals. It's not the elitist system that existed when our country was founded, but it might as well be: a tiny percentage of Americans call the shots.

We understand it, and we don't like it. In 1997, the Pew Charitable Trusts funded a poll asking folks how they felt about Congress, campaign finance, and money-in-politics. The results were reported in the July 15, 1997 issue of "Capital Eye", a publication of the Center for Responsive Politics, a Washington, D.C., watchdog group. Here's what they found. A majority of Americans, Democrats, Republicans, and Independents, felt that:

- Campaign finance reform should be given high priority this year (1997). (It wasn't.)

- Questionable fund raising happens in all or most campaigns.

- Elected officials care more about getting re-elected than doing what's best for the country.

- Good people are discouraged from running for office by the high cost of campaigns.

- Political contributions have too much influence on elections and government policy.

- Elected officials seek or receive political contributions while making decisions about issues of concern to those giving money.

- The use of money often buys political influence in Washington by giving one group more influence, by keeping another from having its say, and by determining election outcomes.

*Running
Politics, Power, and the Press*

For all of Americans' talk about having the oldest and greatest democracy in the world, many other countries do a better job of carrying out their national elections than we do.

A booklet entitled "The World of Campaign Finance," produced by the Center for a New Democracy and The Center for Responsive Politics and co-authored by Joel Rogers and Ellen Miller, reports that *every* industrialized country does it better than we do. Of the 20 nations they studied, every one but our own provides at least some level of public financing of their national elections, either in terms of direct, monetary aid to the political parties, or to the campaigns themselves, or through tax benefits, or through free media time — and media time, of course, is the single largest expense in any U.S. election campaign. In 15 of the 20 countries studied, paid political advertisements on TV are prohibited. And in most of those 20 countries, there are government-imposed limitations on either campaign spending or campaign contributions. In the U.K. for example, election campaigns are limited to six weeks in duration, and candidates for Parliament are given $15,000 in federal money along with free TV time with which to run their campaigns, and all private contributions are prohibited! The table below is taken from "The World of Campaign Finance", and it summarizes the findings.

TABLE 1. Summary of Comparative Political Financing Practices

		Public Financing					Restrictions	
		Campaigns	Parties	Party-affiliated Organizations	Tax Benefits	Media	Spending	Contributions
Campaign Funding Only	Australia	•			•	•		
	Canada	•			•	•	•	
Double Funding	Austria	•	•	•		•		
	France	•	•		•	•	•	•
	Germany	•	•	•	•	•		
	Israel	•	•			•	•	
	Italy	•	•			•		
	Spain	•	•			•	•	•
Scandinavian Model	Belgium		•		•	•	•	
	Denmark		•	•		•		
	Finland		•	•		•		
	Norway		•	•		•		
	Sweden		•	•		•		
The Dutch Exception	Netherlands			•	•	•		
Private Funding Model	Ireland					•		
	Japan					•	•	•
	New Zealand					•	•	
	Switzerland					•		
	United Kingdom					•	•	
United States	President	•					•	•
	Congress							•

In our national turmoil over corrupt campaign practices, many Americans have turned to term limits as the solution. Indeed, a national term limits organization has been in existence in Washington, D.C., for several years. Absent real reform, term limits make sense. Some twenty states have adopted term limits for their legislatures—all by initiative, of course. (There's nothing that we in the states can do to limit congressional terms, unfortunately. Those terms are established by the U.S. Constitution.) Many of those new laws have been challenged in the courts, by both liberal and conservative groups. As a rule, the term-limit initiatives have not fared well against those challenges.

Campaign finance reform hasn't been enacted in our country for want of trying. What reformers keep running into is the freedom of speech clause in the First Amendment to the U.S. Constitution, and the manner in which the U.S. Supreme Court has interpreted "freedom of speech." In the now-infamous *Buckley vs. Valeo* Supreme Court decision of 1976, the Court ruled that to limit campaign *expenditures* was tantamount to limiting the candidate's ability to reach the voters, that is, her or his freedom of speech. The Court never explicitly said that "money equals freedom of speech" and they did allow, in the same decision, a limitation on campaign *contributions* from individuals to $1000 per election. It was a recognition of the fact that candidates just might be bought. Since that Court ruling, elections have become so expensive and clever lawyers and campaign operatives have become so good at finding and exploiting loopholes in the law (soft money, bundling, etc.) that the flow of money is now essentially unlimited. In the '96 federal elections, congressional and presidential candidates raised and spent $2.4 billion. In 2000, that figure rose to $3 billion.

It has been suggested that we amend the U.S. Constitution to break the link between money and free speech. Without attempting to judge the merits of that idea, it should be noted that the Constitution is extremely difficult to amend, another legacy of the Founding Fathers. The Constitution is so difficult to change that—discounting the first 10 amendments known as the Bill of Rights—it has only been amended 17 times in more than 200 years, even though thousands of amendments have been proposed by Congress.

So how do we fix campaign finance and strengthen our democracy? This much is clear: it won't be easy. Still, a number of public interest groups and courageous individuals are trying. Here are some of the leaders in the movement:

1. *Common Cause.* Founded in 1970 by patriot John Gardner, Common Cause is one of the oldest of the good-government organizations in Washington, D.C. It is a nationwide membership organization with more than 250,000 dues-paying members in 40 states. Common Cause involves itself in a number of public-interest issues, but campaign finance reform has always been at or near the top of their list. Originally dedicated to pure public financing of federal election campaigns, they have backed off in recent years because of the intransigence of one Congress after another on this issue. They now favor milder measures such as the several variations of the McCain-Feingold reform bill that would prohibit soft money. In 1997, Common Cause got more than a million people across the country to sign on to the principle of genuine campaign finance reform. When a piece of legislation important to their issues is in Congress, Common Cause has the capacity to put 50 or more volunteers on the phones in their War Room to phone members in special congressional districts to elicit letters and phone calls to members' offices from their constituents. They routinely do 250,000-piece mailings.

   In terms of clout, Common Cause is probably No. 1 in the country.

2. *Public Citizen.* One of several public-interest organizations founded by Ralph Nader, Public Citizen has 100,000 dues-paying members across the country. Public Citizen believes that only incrementalism on campaign finance reform will work: only a Congress elected under revised and tightened election fund-raising rules will act to tighten the rules still further ... and so on, until true campaign finance reform is achieved. There are no facts on the table to prove them wrong. Public Citizen has put out a series of reports on money in politics, and they maintain a Congress Watch office as a watchdog arm.

3. *The Center for Responsive Politics.* The Center for Responsive Politics was started in 1983 by Senators Frank Church of Idaho

and Hugh Scott of Pennsylvania. The Center has done more research on money in politics than any other organization in the country, much of their information coming directly from the Federal Election Commission. The Center for Responsive Politics is not a membership organization; their funding comes mainly from foundations. They don't lobby or take positions on legislation, in order to maintain their neutrality and, with it, their credibility.

4. *The Center for Public Integrity.* This is another non-profit, foundation-funded watchdog group located in Washington, D.C. Founded in 1989, it is staffed with some of the finest investigative reporters in the country, many of them ex-TV news people. Their growing list of investigative reports and books includes "The Buying of the President," "The Buying of the Congress," and "The Buying of the President 2000," all by executive director Charles Lewis and staff.

5. *The PIRGs, Public Interest Research Groups.* The PIRGs are another creation of Ralph Nader. PIRGs exist on about 100 college campuses across the country, taking on consumer and public-interest issues such as plastics recycling, consumer protection, and clean government. USPIRG is the Washington, D.C., organization that loosely binds the state PIRGs into a confederation. USPIRG favors a Constitutional amendment to limit campaign contributions and spending in the longer term, but believes that that can best be achieved by incrementalism, beginning with $100 contribution limits. The PIRGS are perhaps most notable for their ability to put canvassers on the street gathering signatures for statewide initiatives. The director of their Democracy Campaign, Derek Cressman, puts out regular "Political Reform Updates," with news of state actions around the country.

6. *Alliance for Better Campaigns.* This group, formed in 1995 by former Washington Post reporter Paul Taylor, has one immediate goal: to get the commercial TV networks to devote blocks of free time to presidential candidates to get their message to the American voters—not for debates, but for "straight talk". The

Coalition, now co-chaired by Jimmy Carter, Walter Cronkite, and Gerald Ford, feels that the TV time should be blocked, so that all the channels are carrying the message at the same time, to avoid losing the channel surfers. And, as Step 2, they advocate the same free TV time for congressional candidates. Foundation-funded, the Alliance met with limited success in the '96 and 2000 federal elections.

7. *The National Voting Rights Institute.* This Boston-based organization was created in 1994 by John Bonifaz. It is foundation-funded and non-profit, and engages in legal challenges, instead of moving public opinion, in opposition to the money-driven election process. Their trump card, they believe, is the 14th Amendment, which guarantees equal protection under the law to all citizens. They believe that as long as corporate and PAC money runs the show, the rest of us have lost our equal protection. A few of the Institute's early cases have been decided unfavorably for The People; others are in the works.

8. *The Campaign Reform Project.* Jerry Kohlberg of Kohlberg-Kravis-Roberts fame has dedicated several million dollars of his personal wealth to help bring about campaign finance reform. Their approach appears to be incremental — to begin in one or two Congressional districts — and their most visible activity to date has been some national newspaper ads.

9. *Public Campaign.* This is the newest of the national campaign finance reform organizations. It was created in the mid-'90s by Ellen Miller, who for several years directed the Center for Responsive Politics. Perhaps, ultimately, it will prove to be the most successful. Public Campaign raised almost $10 million from foundations and has endorsed "Clean Money Campaign Reform", in which candidates for in-state offices (not Congress, unfortunately) who reject all private money are supplied with adequate public money to fund their campaign. Maine, Massachusetts, and Arizona passed clean money initiatives in 1996 and 1998, and the Vermont Legislature passed a similar statute in 1997. "Clean Money" elections took place in those states

in 2000, with positive results. Unfortunately, similar initiatives in Missouri and Oregon failed in 2000.

10. *The Alliance for Democracy.* The Alliance was created in the mid-'90s by former Texas Observer editor Ronnie Dugger. It describes itself as a progressive national movement. It's not a political party, although it may become one some day. For now, it's a growing group of people across the country disaffected with both major political parties and their platforms. Among other changes in our society, they want to end corporate personhood, reduce corporate welfare, change the U.S. Constitution, fight economic insecurity, and, of course, effect campaign finance reform.

11. *Regional and other Groups.* There are several groups, including NECARC, the New England Citizen Action Research Center, dedicated to a number of public interest issues such as affordable housing and progressive taxes. Campaign finance reform is naturally one of their key objectives. ACORN, the Association of Community Organizations for Reform Now, is located in a number of states and has a similar plateful of issues. They, too, have made genuine campaign finance reform one of their primary issues.

12. *New Political Parties.* Any new political party recognizes that it hasn't a prayer of electing anyone to a major office as long as Big Money is dominant, and so campaign finance reform is high on all of their agendas: the New Party, the evolving Labor Party, the Green Party, etc.

13. *Ad Hoc Groups.* Local organizations spring up all the time to advocate for campaign finance reform initiatives in their states. The states with the most active groups include California, Colorado, Minnesota, Montana, New Jersey, North Carolina, Oregon, and Wisconsin.

14. *The League of Women Voters.* A huge national membership organization that has made campaign finance reform one of its principal issues.

15. *Still Others*. The Center for Voting and Democracy, a Washington, D.C. group chaired by 1980 independent presidential candidate John Anderson, champions proportional representation, along with campaign finance reform. Progressive Communication Systems of Madison, WI created a national road-show featuring populist Jim Hightower and former U.S. Senate candidate Ed Garvey to bring campaign finance reform issues down home. The Advocacy Institute of Washington, D.C., puts out advisories and talking points on a number of issues, including money-in-politics. The Campaign for America's Future is yet another Washington, D.C., organization creating public debate on economic and social policies for improving the lives of working Americans; campaign finance reform is on their agenda, too, naturally.

Thus there are more than a dozen organizations, many of them national with large memberships and money-raising ability, all fighting for campaign finance reform. (Contact information for these organizations is presented in Appendix B.)

The reform effort continues to be a case of "two steps forward and one back." Two case studies are noteworthy. In 1994 in Oregon, a coalition of groups including Common Cause, the state PIRG, and the League of Women Voters placed a campaign finance reform initiative on the ballot calling for contribution limits of $100 for legislative elections as well as spending limits for all statewide and legislative elections. The initiative was approved by the voters overwhelmingly: 72% voted "Yes." Unfortunately, the Oregon Supreme Court ruled much of the new law unconstitutional in 1996 and the $100 limits no longer apply. While they were in effect, however, campaign spending in Oregon elections took a major dip, the first such drop in years. Otherwise, it has been up, up, up! And that is just what happened again in the '98 and 2000 election cycles.

In 1996, a statewide "Clean Money" campaign finance reform initiative passed in Maine. The Maine initiative achieved ballot status when a coalition of AARP, Common Cause, the AFL-CIO, the League of Women Voters, and others produced a hard core of 1100 volunteers who gathered the required 65,000+ signatures in one 14-hour period! That accomplishment may well be unique in American history. And the initiative passed. The new law provides public funding for all statewide and legislative elections in Maine, at levels that allow the candidates to get their message to the voters without raising taxes. The funding comes from higher fees on lobbyists, a small reduction in the cost of running the state legislature, and a tax check-off. Any candidate accepting the public money has to agree to accept no private money. But candidates are not required to take public money, and millionaires, for example, can still fund their own campaigns. The new law is thus not coercive and has withstood constitutional challenge. Unfortunately, as noted, similar initiatives went down to defeat in Missouri and Oregon in 2000, in spite of well-organized and well-funded campaigns.

In spite of those setbacks, the long term strategy, shared by the best informed campaign finance reform people, is to pass laws like the Maine law in as many states as possible over the next several years, either by initiative or by action of the state legislatures. The expectation then is that, with continued pressure applied to the U.S. Congress by the public interest groups and their members, Congress will finally realize that we mean it, and will enact real reform at the federal level.

Compared with the pork, boondoggles, tax breaks, military waste, and corporate welfare that we now suffer through, and the costs thereof, publicly funded elections at the federal level would be an enormous bargain. It has been estimated that the cost of all federal elections, even if the entire cost were passed on to the taxpayers, would be no more than $5 per taxpayer per year. The average taxpayer pays more than that for one Seawolf submarine or one B-2 bomber.

But campaign finance reform at the federal level won't be easy, no matter how many states pass campaign finance reform laws. What we're really asking the members of Congress to do is to run their re-election campaigns on a nearly level playing field ("nearly" because the incumbent almost always has the advantage of name familiarity), and thus put their very jobs at risk.

And just who will lead the charge on genuine campaign finance reform at the federal level? Thus far, Senators John McCain and Russ Feingold are leading it, along with House members Marty Meehan and Chris Shays. Their draft legislation would eliminate all soft money and also eliminate so-called "issue ads" that are actually candidate ads in disguise. But who knows what their legislation will look like once both houses of Congress get through with it and President Bush signs it (if he does) into law? And even the McCain-Feingold legislation doesn't touch the enormous flow of "hard money" from PACs, individuals, and other special interests, nor does it affect so-called independent expenditures. Even those members of Congress favorably disposed to reform wouldn't agree to rejecting the Big Money unless their opponent did, too. They see it as unilateral disarmament.

To add to the difficulties, we have prominent lawmakers, those who have a national voice, calling for *anti*-reform. Kentucky Senator Mitch McConnell and others point out, correctly, that as a nation we spend more on toothpaste or antacid commercials than we do on political campaigns. They want *more* money involved in elections.

Still others say that the solution is simply to require full and prompt disclosure of the sources of campaign contributions. They claim that would put the full public spotlight on any corruption and tend to dissuade any monkey business. But that argument is hogwash. Most Americans, including the vast majority who actually decide election outcomes, probably wouldn't bother to read about it if it were on the front page of their daily newspaper. And if everyone's taking the money, whom do you punish?

# # #

What can we as individuals do to, in the words made famous by Ross Perot, "take our country back?" Well, there are several small things that each of us can do that would help: agitate!; write letters to the editor of the local newspaper (and the national newspapers, too); get better informed by reading and talking with informed friends; attend those town hall meetings our Congresspeople put on regularly back in the district, and ask where *their* money comes from and what they're doing to enact genuine campaign finance reform; run for office, if that's a possibility; form a campaign finance reform group in your community; join one of the national or local organizations dedicated to true campaign finance reform; and perhaps even visit your Congressperson and your Senators back in Washington, D.C., and talk seriously with them about your concerns and about the need for campaign finance reform. All of the great movements in our nation's history — ending slavery, civil rights,

Harry Lonsdale

Toles ©1996 The Buffalo News. Reprinted with permission of Universal Press Syndicate. All rights reserved.

women's suffrage, the end of the Vietnam War, the nuclear test ban, and more—came about after long struggles by The People, and success wasn't achieved in many cases until the twilight of those struggles, after many of the early activists had burned out and moved on.

I continue to hope that someone who cares deeply about this country, is deeply concerned about our corrupt elections process, who has the capacity to write a few $1 million checks and is willing to do so, will identify a small handful of opponents of real campaign finance reform in the Congress and will spend sufficient money in the form of independent expenditures to defeat those reform opponents at the polls. A million bucks, well placed, will defeat darn near anyone in Congress. Even our toughest opponents can be knocked out with less than $5 million. And the knockout punch has to be based on the campaign finance reform message, and it has be applied through those same, vacuous 30-second TV spots that candidates win elections with.

The messages would have to be delivered several times a day on each TV station in the Congressperson's district, and repeated often enough that the average voter sees them multiple times, so that the message is imprinted. That's exactly how the politicians got elected in the first place. What could be more fitting than to turn out the opponents of real campaign finance reform with the same rotten rules the incumbents passed to keep themselves in power! Hey, it's just free speech!

I believe that it would work. And when we defeat one or two or three incumbents this way, the rest will get the message. Indeed, it may be the *only* way they will get the message.

# # #

Perhaps the most important lesson for me from my three Senate campaigns has been that a lot of people, spread across this country, truly believe in the ideal that is America. They believe in our Declaration of Independence, even if our country hasn't always practiced it. I've been inspired by a number of people who have gone against the grain — some have even gone to jail — to try to make this country a better place.

# # #

I'll close with some inspirational words from Margaret Mead:

"Never doubt that a small group of thoughtful, committed citizens can change the world; indeed it's the only thing that ever has."

Harry Lonsdale

EPILOGUE

More than a decade has passed since I first ran for the United States Senate.

In the summer of 2001, people were still going to jail in Oregon for protesting the logging of old-growth forests on public lands.

One U.S. Senate candidate, Democrat Jon Corzine of New Jersey, spent $63 million on his campaign in 2000—$40 million of it on TV ads—an all-time record amount (so far). He outspent his opponent 10 to one, and won, of course.

In 2001, the people of Great Britain elected their *entire parliament* for only $60 million. Paid political ads are not allowed in Britain.

Meanwhile, the U.S. Congress continued to wrestle with campaign finance reform. In 2001, the Senate passed the McCain-Feingold bill, which would prohibit all soft-money contributions and disallow phony "issue ads." And, after much arm-twisting, the House of Representatives passed a similar piece of legislation, known as the Shays-Meehan bill. My wife and I were sitting in the House gallery on the day the bill was debated and passed, Feb. 13, 2002.

As I write this, in March 2002, the two houses of Congress have not yet sent the bill to the president for his signature, and President Bush hasn't indicated whether he will veto it or sign it and take credit.

But even if McCain-Feingold-Shays-Meehan becomes law and withstands the threatened court challenges, it won't end the corruption. The system will remain awash with money to pay for those expensive TV ads in election campaigns. Only free TV time or publicly funded elections will clean up the mess and, perhaps, restore our confidence in Congress.

Harry Lonsdale

Appendix A

Mark Hatfield's Fund Raising

Serving in the United States Senate means a lot more than just giving those sometimes-eloquent speeches on the Senate floor that we see on C-SPAN; more than casting votes on the vital issues of the day, affecting Supreme Court nominations, or going to war; more than meeting constituents back home, or in the Senate office — it means, if the Senator hopes to get re-elected, raising money, lots of it. It has been estimated that a U.S. Senator from a large state must raise an average of $5000 a day, every day, for her or his entire six-year term in order to be able to afford television ads and the other expenses inherent in the next election. As one who spent three hours a day, six days a week for months on end, trying to raise money for my own Senate campaigns, I can attest to the fact that fund raising is an extraordinarily difficult and time-consuming activity, at least for challengers.

It's easier for incumbents, of course, and especially for powerfully positioned incumbents like Mark Hatfield who served on the Senate Appropriations Committee for many years, being both committee chair and ranking member at various times. When it comes to fund raising, Appropriations is the honey pot of committees; after all, those two dozen or so committee members dole out almost two *trillion* dollars of taxpayer money every year. Hatfield also served on the Energy and Natural Resources Committee, which dealt with public lands, our national parks and forests, and water and power issues. And, of course, he had the opportunity to vote on *every* issue that came before the Senate.

Hatfield spent about $2.75 million on the 1990 Senate race (we spent $1.48 million, most of it my own money). More than $1 million of Hatfield's campaign contributions came from Political Action Committees (PACs); we accepted no PAC money. Another $900,000 came from individuals who contributed $200 or more, so-called "large contributors." Counting contributions from the Republican Party, more than 80% of his contributions came from PACs, large contributors, or the Republican Party; only 11% came from small individual contributors, those who contributed less than $200. Almost half of his large individual contributions came from outside of Oregon. More than 80% of his PAC contributions came from business PACs. (This information, as well as the compilation in Table A-1 below, came from the Center for Responsive Politics in Washington, D.C., which keeps close tabs on contributions and expenditures of every member of Congress, including challengers, each election cycle.)

The PAC contributions to Hatfield's 1990 Senate race are listed in Table A-1. Only contributors of $1000 or more are listed, and the list of contributors is broken down into a dozen or more categories: Agriculture, Construction, Communications/Electronics, etc. I have chosen to list PAC contributions because I feel these are particularly egregious contributions, really being nothing more than legalized bribes. Individuals are limited to $1000 contributions per election cycle and there is at least the possibility that individual contributors are old friends, or people who want clean government. With PACs, however, you *know* they want something when the election is over, and their contribution limit is $5000 per election cycle (primary plus general election) or $10,000 per election.

Table A-1 consists of more than 350 PACs that contributed $1000 or more (another 80 PACs contributed less than $1000). Several of those PACs contributed the legal limit of $10,000. Most of the PACs are unknown to you and me, most of them don't come from Oregon, and many of them don't even represent Oregonians. But they all have interests in the business of the U.S. Senate.

At first glance it would appear that every corporate and private interest in America is represented in that long list. Not so. Environmental organizations, many of whom have PACs, are noticeably absent, as is NARAL, the National Abortion Rights Action League. Interestingly, both Handgun Control, Inc. and the National Rifle Association contributed to Hatfield's 1990 election campaign.

Two organizations not listed in Table A-1 made "independent expenditures" toward Hatfield's campaign: the National Committee to Preserve Social Security ($25,000) and the National Right to Life PAC ($22,000). There has been a dramatic increase in independent expenditure campaigns in federal elections since 1990; in some cases, independent expenditures can now *exceed* the candidate's expenditures.

Labor unions contributed about one-tenth of Hatfield's PAC contributions. That's surprising in view of the fact that he was a

Republican with a mediocre voting record on labor issues, such as the minimum wage. Apparently, the unions felt more comfortable with a "bird in the hand." Labor union contribution decisions are not made by the complete union membership, but rather by a tiny finance or steering committee. Nor are union members as predominantly Democratic as in years past. There have been increasing efforts in recent years to pass laws that would require that written authorization be obtained from union members before their political contributions are allocated to candidates. Those efforts to date, by voter initiatives in California, Oregon, and other states, as well as in the U.S. Congress, have failed, but the issue is far from dead.

Individuals affiliated with the timber industry contributed handsomely to Hatfield's campaign. Shown in Table A-2 are more than 100 individuals, and the timber-related companies they represented, who contributed, several of them more than once. Altogether, they contributed $100,000, in addition to the more than $60,000 in PAC money that the timber industry contributed. The individuals in Table A-2 are a Who's Who of the Oregon timber industry. The list was compiled by an industrious member of our 1990 campaign staff from Federal Election Commission reports, and it can best be considered only a partial list, because the affiliations of many contributors (listed as "Housewife," etc.) are frequently impossible to trace.

As we noted in Chapter 2, the 1990 Senate race got very close during the final few weeks. One of the polls even had us ahead with about three weeks to go. At that point, the Hatfield campaign pulled out all the stops in their fund-raising effort. Somebody — Hatfield?, Gerry Frank? Elaine Franklin? — was working the phones virtually around the clock. The evidence is found in their reports to the F.E.C., which requires that all contributions of $1000 or more must be reported with 48 hours during the last three weeks of the campaign. The Hatfield campaign took in an average of over $30,000 *a day* over those last three weeks, most of it from people far from Oregon, or from PACs you've never heard of, and almost every dollar of it was spent on television ads. Meanwhile, over in our shop, we considered it a great day when a single $1000 check arrived. I know from my own experience that Hatfield's checks didn't just show up in the mail. They were solicited, and probably solicited *hard*. Every one of those contributors was called at least once, and a lot more were presumably called who declined to contribute.

Harry Lonsdale

The final insult to my sensibilities came from politicians who contributed to Hatfield's campaign from their own campaign funds. It's another scam that's been going on for many years: one Senator will contribute to another who may be in a close election, to pay back previous favors or to lay the groundwork for future favors. Among Hatfield's $1000 contributors were Citizens for (Senator Thad) Cochran, Jake Garn Re-election Committee, Jeffords for Vermont Committee, McClure for U.S. Senator Committee, Nickles for U.S. Senate, People for Pete Domenici Committee, Re-elect Packwood Committee, Senator Larry Pressler, Steve Symms for Senate, Conrad Burns/U.S. Senate, Dan Coats for Indiana, Friends for Slade Gorton, Friends of Phil Gramm, Friends of Connie Mack, John McCain for Re-election Committee, Kansans for Kassebaum, as well as "friends of" Senator John Heinz, Frank Murkowski, Strom Thurmond, John Chafee, John Warner, Alan Simpson, Ted Stevens, and Malcolm Wallop, as well as some members of the Oregon State Legislature. About the only people who *didn't* contribute to Hatfield's campaign were 3-1/2 million Oregonians.

In the end, we probably had more individual contributors (5000+) to our campaign than Hatfield did to his, but our average contribution was less than $100, no match for Hatfield's $3000+ average PAC contribution.

What are we to make of all of those $1000-and-up contributions to Hatfield? What did they get for all their money? Did they buy him? Certainly not directly; bribing government officials is still a criminal offense. But they certainly bought access and a sympathetic ear on their issues. Trying to tie campaign contributions to specific votes, or the suppression of votes, is a nearly impossible task. One would have to be a mind reader. All we have, really, is the perception of corruption.

Finally, in presenting this long list of contributions, I'm not insinuating that Mark Hatfield broke any laws or that his fund raising was any more obscene than that of his 534 colleagues then in the Congress. I *am* saying that the laws are obscene and that Congress should clean up its act. Every American citizen has three representatives in Congress: one member of the House and two Senators. Whatever state you're from and whatever time of day you're reading this, the chances are good that one of your three representatives is on the phone right now, asking for campaign contributions.

Table A-1

Hatfield's PAC Contributions
1990 Senate Campaign

AGRICULTURE

    American Association of Nurserymen, $2,000
    American Bakers Association, $2,000
    American Crystal Sugar Corporation, $1,000
    American Veterinary Medical Association, $1,000
    Archer-Daniels-Midland Corporation, $2,500
    Boise Cascade, $5,000
    Champion International Corporation, $5,000
    Con-Agra Inc., $5,000
    Dairymen Inc., $1,000
    Darigold/Northwest Dairymens Association, $2,000
    Deere & Company, $1,000
    Flowers Industries, $5,000
    Food Marketing Institute, $3,000
    Georgia-Pacific Corporation, $9,000
    International Paper Company, $9,000
    James River Corporation of Virginia, $2,000
    Manville Corporation, $1,000
    Mead Corporation, $1,000
    Milk Industry Foundation, $2,000
    Multnomah Plywood, $1,000
    Nabisco Brands, Inc., $1,000
    National Broiler Council, $1,000
    National Cattlemen's Association, $1,000
    National Cotton Council, $2,000
    National Council of Farmer Co-ops, $1,000
    National Forest Products Association, $4,500
    Ocean Spray Cranberries, Inc., $6,000
    Quaker Oats, $1,000
    Roseburg Lumber Company, $2,000
    Scott Paper Company, $1,000

Simpson Investment Company, $6,000
Southern Minnesota Beet Sugar Co-op, $2,250
Sun Studs Inc., $4,000
Union Camp Corporation, $2,500
Weyerhaeuser Company, $6,500
Willamette Industries, $6,000

CONSTRUCTION

American Consulting Engineers Council, $3,000
American Supply Association, $1,000
Associated Builders & Contractors, $1,000
Associated General Contractors, $10,000
CH2M Hill, $1,928
Caterpillar Tractor, $1,000
Fibreboard Corporation, $1,000
Jacobs Engineering Group, $1,000
National Association of Home Builders, $7,000
National Electrical Contractors Association, $2,000
National Society of Professional Engineers, $2,000
National Utility Contractors Association, $5,000
Owens-Corning Fiberglas, $3,000
Parsons Corporation, $1,000
Photogrammetric Surveyors Management Association, $1,000
Sheet Metal/Air Conditioning Contractors, $1,000

COMMUNICATIONS/ELECTRONICS

AT&T, $8,000
Association of American Publishers, $1,000
ASCAP, $1,000
Bell Atlantic, $3,500
BellSouth Corp., $3,500
BellSouth Services, $2,000
Comsat, $1,000
Contel, $1,000
Fox Inc., $1,000
Intel Corporation, $3,000
MCA Inc., $2,300

MCI Telecommunications, $1,500
McCaw Cellular Communications, $2,000
Motion Picture Association of America, $1,000
National Association of Broadcasters, $6,000
National Cable Television Association, $10,000
NYNEX Corporation, $3,000
Pacific Northwest Bell, $2,000
Pacific Telesis Group, $3,000
RR Donnelley & Sons, $2,000
Southwestern Bell, $2,000
U.S. West Inc., $8,000
United Telecommunications, $5,000
Walt Disney Company, $2,000
West Publishing, $1,000

DEFENSE

Allied Signal, $3,000
American Systems Corporation, $1,000
Atlantic Research Corporation, $1,000
Avondale Industries, $1,000
Boeing Company, $3,000
Chrysler Corporation, $2,000
Computer Sciences Corporation, $1,000
FMC Corporation, $1,000
GTE Corporation, $4,000
Gencorp Inc., $3,000
General Atomics, $3,000
General Dynamics, $1,000
General Electric, $4,000
General Motors, $1,000
Grumman, $1,000
Hughes Aircraft, $2,000
ITT Corporation, $1,000
Litton Industries, $3,000
Lockheed Corporation, $1,000
Martin Marietta Corporation, $3,000
McDonnell Douglas, $2,000

McDonnell Douglas Helicopter, $2,000
Morrison-Knudsen, $1,000
Motorola Inc., $1,000
Rockwell International, $2,500
Sea-Land Corporation, $3,500
TRW Inc., $1,000
Tektronix Inc., $1,000
Textron Inc., $4,000
UNC Inc., $2,000
United Technologies, $5,000

ENERGY & NATURAL RESOURCES

ACRE-Action Committee/Rural Electrification, $6,000
Alcoa, $1,000
American Gas Association, $1,000
American Public Power Association, $1,250
Amoco Corporation, $5,000
Atlantic Richfield, $2,250
BHP-Utah International, $1,000
BP America, $3,000
Babcock & Wilcox, $1,000
Batelle Memorial Institute, $1,000
Brown & Root, $2,000
CH2M Hill, $5,000
CBI Industries, $1,000
Chevron Corporation, $7,000
Columbia Natural Resources, $2,000
Cooper Industries, $5,000
Detroit Edison, $1,000
Enserch Corporation, $1,000
Exxon Corporation, $5,000
Fluor Corporation, $5,000
Freeport-McRoRan Inc., $1,000
Idaho Power Company, $1,000
Internorth Inc., $1,000
Interstate Natural Gas Association, $1,250
Kaiser Aluminum & Chemical, $1,000

Louisiana Land & Exploration, $1,000
Mapco Inc., $2,000
National Coal Association, $4,000
Nerco Inc. (Oregon), $2,500
Northwest Natural Gas, $1,250
Occidental Oil & Gas, $1,000
Occidental Petroleum, $2,000
Oryx Energy Co., $1,000
Pacific Enterprises, $3,000
Pacific Gas & Electric, $2,000
Pacific Power & Light, $4,000
Peabody Coal, $1,000
Pennzoil Company, $2,000
Petroleum Marketers Association, $5,000
Philadelphia Electric Company, $1,000
Pittston Company, $1,000
Portland General Electric Company, $3,000
Public Service Company of New Mexico, $1,000
Reynolds Metals, $5,000
Santa Fe International Corporation, $2,000
Shell Oil, $3,500
Southern California Edison, $1,500
Southland Corporation, $1,007
Sun Company, $1,000
Texaco, $1,000
Union Pacific Corporation, $8,000
WR Grace & Company, $1,000
Waste Management Inc., $6,000
Williams Companies, $2,000

FINANCE, INSURANCE & REAL ESTATE

Aetna Life & Casualty, $3,000
American Bankers Association, $10,000
American Council of Life Insurance, $3,000
American Family Corporation, $6,000
American Financial Services Association, $1,000
American International Group, $3,000

American Land Title Association, $1,000
American Security Bank, $4,500
Arthur Anderson & Company, $1,000
BankAmerica, $2,500
Barnett Banks of Florida, $2,000
Benjamin Franklin Federal Savings & Loan, $2,000
Blue Cross/Blue Shield, $2,381
Chevy Chase Savings Bank, $2,000
Chicago Board of Trade, $5,000
Chicago Mercantile Exchange, $5,000
Citicorp, $2,500
Credit Union National Association, $2,500
Delta Dental Plan Association, $1,000
Federated Investors Inc., $1,000
First Interstate Bank/Oregon, $3,000
Great Western Financial Corporation, $2,000
Health Insurance Association of America, $2,000
Independent Insurance Agents of America, $2,000
Investment Company Institute, $1,000
Irvine Company, $1,000
Liberty Mutual Insurance, $2,500
Manufacturers Hanover, $1,000
Marine Midland Banks, $1,000
Merrill Lynch, $2,000
Metropolitan Life Insurance, $1,000
Mortgage Bankers Association of America, $1,000
National Association of Independent Insurers, $2,000
National Association of Life Underwriters, $6,000
National Association of Professional Insurance Agents, $1,000
National Association of Realtors, $9,550
National Venture Capital Association, $6,000
Northwestern Mutual Life, $2,000
Prudential-Bache Securities, $1,000
Prudential Insurance, $1,000
Salomon Brothers, $7,000
Security Pacific Bank Oregon, $1,000
Security Pacific Corporation, $1,250
Standard Insurance Company, $2,000

Torchmark Corporation, $5,000
Travelers Corporation, $1,000
U.S. Bancorp, $8,200
U.S. Fidelity & Guaranty, $1,000
U.S. League of Savings Associations, $3,500

MISCELLANEOUS BUSINESS

American Hotel & Motel Association, $1,000
Bowling Proprietors Association, $1,000
Business Industry PAC, $2,098
Clorox Company, $1,000
Conference of National Park Concessioners, $1,000
Dun & Bradstreet, $4,000
Footwear Distributors & Retailers of America, $1,000
Fred Meyer Inc., $7,000
General Electric, $1,000
Holiday Corporation, $1,000
International Council of Shopping Centers, $2,000
J.C. Penney Company, $1,000
Marriott Corporation, $1,000
May Department Stores, $2,000
McDonald's Corporation, $5,000
Morrison Inc., $1,000
National Association of Wholesaler-Distributors, $1,000
National Confectioners Association, $1,000
National Machine Tool Builders Association, $1,000
Nike Inc., $8,000
Stone Container Corporation, $5,000

HEALTH

Abbott Laboratories, $3,000
American Academy of Ophthalmology, $6,000
American Association of Nurse Anesthetists, $3,000
American Chiropractic Association, $5,000
American College of Emergency Physicians, $1,000
American Dental Association, $5,000

American Hospital Association, $5,000
American Medical Association, $10,000
American Nurses Association, $1,500
American Optometric Association, $3,000
American Pharmaceutical Association, $1,000
American Physical Therapy Association, $2,000
American Podiatry Association, $2,000
Ansell Inc., $1,000
Association for the Advancement of Psychology, $3,000
Bristol-Myers Squibb, $1,000
Committee for Quality Orthopedic Health Care, $2,000
Corporation for the Advancement of Psychiatry, $2,000
Eli Lilly & Company, $1,000
Federation of American Hospitals, $1,000
McKesson Corporation, $2,000
Merck & Company, $2,000
National Association of Pharmacists, $3,000
Oral & Maxillofacial Surgeons, $3,000
Pfizer Inc., $3,000
Shaklee Corporation, $1,000
Upjohn Company, $4,000

LAWYERS & LOBBYISTS

Baker & Botts, $1,000
Burson-Marsteller, $2,500
Crowell & Moring, $1,000
Davis Wright PAC, $1,000
Dickstein, Shapiro & Morin, $1,500
Dow, Lohnes & Albertson, $2,500
Garvey, Schubert & Barer, $2,000
Hill & Knowlton, $1,000
Kutak, Rock & Campbell, $1,000
Laxalt, Washington et al, $1,000
Manatt, Phelps et al, $2,000
Powell, Goldstein et al, $1,000
Rivkin, Radler, Dunne & Bayh, $1,000
Skadden Arps PAC, $3,000

Stoel, Rives, Boley et al, $5,500
Van Ness, Feldman et al, $1,205
Verner, Liipfert et al, $7,339
Vinson, Elkins, Searls et al, $1,000
Wexler Group, $2,000
Williams & Jensen, $2,000
Wolf, Block, Schorr et al, $1,000

TRANSPORTATION

Aircraft Owners & Pilots Association, $5,000
American Airlines, $1,000
American Commercial Barge Line Company, $1,000
American President Lines, $1,000
American Trucking Associations, $2,000
American Waterways Operators, $1,000
Auto Dealers & Drivers for Free Trade, $7,500
Burlington Northern Railroad, $4,000
Burlington Resources, $3,000
Chicago & North Western Transport, $1,000
Delta Airlines, $4,500
Federal Express Corporation, $9,000
ITEL Corporation, $1,000
Kansas City Southern, $2,000
National Auto Dealers Association, $6,000
Norfolk Southern Corporation, $3,000
Outboard Marine Corporation, $2,000
Paccar Inc., $1,000
Southern Pacific Transportation Company, $1,000
Southwest Marine, $7,000
Texas Air, $7,000
United Airlines, $2,000
United Parcel Service, $7,500
Viking Freight, $1,000

LABOR

Air Line Pilots Association, $10,000
Amalgamated Transit Union, $2,600

American Federation of Government Employees, $1,000
American Federation of State/County/Municipal Employees, $1,000
American Postal Workers Union, $3,000
Carpenters & Joiners Union, $7,500
Food & Commercial Workers Union, $2,500
International Association of Firefighters, $1,500
International Brotherhood of Electrical Workers, $1,000
Ironworkers Union, $5,000
Laborers' Political League, $5,000
Longshoremen's & Warehousemen's Union, $1,000
Machinists/Aerospace Workers Union, $1,000
Marine Engineers Union, $9,000
National Association of Letter Carriers, $7,000
National Association of Postal Supervisors, $1,000
National Association of Retired Federal Employees, $5,000
National Education Association, $7,500
National Association of Postmasters, $3,000
National League of Postmasters, $1,000
National Rural Letter Carriers Association, $3,000
National Treasury Employees Union, $4,527
Oregon Education Association, $2,500
Plumbers/Pipefitters Union, $4,000
Seafarers International Union, $5,000
Teamsters Union, $7,500
Trans Comm International Union, $1,700
United Paperworkers, $1,000
United Transportation Union, $4,000

IDEOLOGICAL-SINGLE ISSUE

American Citizens for Political Action, $1,100
Assembly of Turkish-American Associations, $1,000
Bluegrass Committee, $5,000
Campaign America, $10,000
Capitol Committee, $1,000
Catch the Spirit PAC, $4,000
Council for a Livable World, $5,471
Friends & Advocates of Biomedical Research, $1,000

Fund for a Republican Majority, $4,000
Handgun Control Inc., $3,000
Heartland PAC of Missouri, $3,000
Hellenic American Council, $2,000
Kids PAC, $5,000
National Albanian American PAC, $5,000
National Committee to Preserve Social Security, $7,000
National Community Action Foundation, $12,000
National Rifle Association, $3,000
Republican Majority Fund, $1,500
Senate Victory Fund, $6,000

OTHER

Committee for Farmworker Programs, $1,000
Association of Independent Colleges & Schools, $2,000

Harry Lonsdale

Table A-2

Contributions to Hatfield's 1990 Senate Campaign from Timber-related Individuals

Gerald Ashland	RLK & Company
William Avison	Avison Lumber
Gordon Ball	South Coast Lumber
Robert Ballin	Corroon & Black
Owen Bentley, Jr.	Brand S Corporation
W. R. Berkley	W. R. Berkley Corporation
Michael Berolzheimer	P & M Cedar Products
C. W. Bingham	Weyerhaeuser
Darrel Bonde	South Coast Lumber
John S. Brandis, Jr.	Brand S Corporation
Jerry Bodie	WTD Industries
G. M. Brown	South Coast Lumber
Michael Burrill	Burrill Lumber Company
Elizabeth Cameron	Starker Forest Products
Mr. & Mrs. Leslie Campbell	SDS Lumber
B. H. Carpenter	John Day Lumber
Mr. & Mrs. Matt Chapman	CFI
Mr. & Mrs. John Cheney	SDS Lumber
Paul Cole	Rosboro Lumber
Bruce Daucsavage	Ochoco Lumber
R. J. Dearmond	Idaho Forest
Richard Devenport	Burrill Lumber
Dan Dutton	Stinson Lumber
Robert Ellingson	Ellingson Lumber
Bruce Engel	Glide Lumber
Mark Fleming	Bald-Knob Land & Timber
Allyn Ford	Roseburg Lumber
Sally Ford	Roseburg Lumber
Rob Freres	Freres Lumber
James Geisinger	Northwest Forestry Association
Richard Gervais	Chiloquin Forest
John R. Gilbertson	Alpine Veneers Inc.
A. B. Hallstrom	Zip-o-Log Mills
James Hallstrom	Zip-o-Log Mills
Karl Hallstrom	Zip-o-Log Mills
William Hallstrom	Zip-o-Log Mills
David Hampton	Hampton Tree Farm
Carol Hampton	Hampton Tree Farm

Harry Lonsdale

John Hampton	Willamina Lumber
David Hancock	Hancock Lumber
Mr. & Mrs. Sterling Hanel	Hanel Lumber
Mr. & Mrs. Milton Herbert	Sawmill Owners
G. A. Hertrich	Vanport Manufacturing
Andrew Honzel	Columbia Plywood
Lawrence Hull	South Coast Lumber
Letha Hull	South Coast Lumber
Ralph Hull	Hull-Oakes Lumber
Curtis Johnson	Burrill Lumber
Don R. Johnson	D. R. Johnson Lumber
Everett Johnson	C & D Lumber
Jody Jones	Seneca Sawmill
Josephine Forest Products	
Dan Keller	Keller Lumber
John Keller	Keller Lumber
R. B. Keller	Keller Enterprises
Sam Konnie	Swanson Brothers Lumber
Lewis Krauss	Rough & Ready Lumber
Gus Kuehne	Northwest Independent Forests
William Lindsey	Rosboro Lumber
Joseph McCracken	Western Forest Industries
Mr. & Mrs. Paul McCracken	Tumac Lumber
Sidney McVay	South Coast Lumber
Thomas Mehl	Gregory Forest Products
Harold Miller	Associated Oregon Loggers
James Miller	South Coast Lumber
Lester Olsen	South Coast Lumber
John O'Neill	RLK & Company
Michael Onustock	Willamette Industries
Tom Partin	Malheur Lumber
Jack Patrick	Patrick Lumber
Strayer Pittman	Bohemia
Mr. & Mrs. Peter Pope	Pope & Talbot
Robert Ragon	Sun Studs
Anita Reynolds	Josephine Forest Products
Foster Robinson	Stanfine Lumber
James Rowe	Brand S Corporation
SDS Lumber	
Louis Samon	Rosboro Lumber
Darrell Schroeder	Stimson Lumber

Thomas Shaw	Modoc Lumber
Linda Shelk	Ochoco Lumber
Stewart Shelk	Ochoco Lumber
Stuart Shelk	Ochoco Lumber
Charles Shotts	Gilchrist Timber
F. W. Smith	Coos Head Lumber
E. L. Spalding	Josephine Forest Products
Merwin Spalding	Josephine Forest Products
Anne Stevenson	SDS Lumber
Bruce Stevenson	SDS Lumber
Mark Stevenson	SDS Lumber
Wallace Stevenson	SDS Lumber
Fred Sohn	Sun Studs
Howard Sohn	Lone Rock Timber
Richard Sohn	Sun Studs
Robert Spence	Pacific Lumber & Shipping
Dennis Spencer	Fort Vancouver Plywood
B. Bond Starker	Starker Forest Products
Barte Starker	Starker Forest Products
Marilyn Starker	Starker Forest Products
Charles Stensrud	Brazier Forest
John Stephens	Roseburg Lumber
L. L. "Stub" Stewart	Bohemia Lumber
James Stock	Clear Lumber
Peter Stott	Crown Pacific
Mr. & Mrs. Bruce Summers	Taylor Lumber & Tree
Ann Swindells	Willamette Industries
George Swindells	Fairway Western
Helen Swindells	Willamette Industries
Susan Hawes Swindells	Willamette Industries
William Swindells	Willamette Industries
George Weyerhauser	Weyerhaeuser
Wendy Weyerhauser	Weyerhaeuser
Scott Williams	Murphy Creek Lumber
Ronald Yanke	R-Y Timber Inc.

Harry Lonsdale

Appendix B

CAMPAIGN FINANCE REFORM AND GOOD-GOVERNMENT ORGANIZATIONS

ACORN
Steve Kest, Executive Director
738 8th St SE
Washington DC 20003
(202) 547-2500
www.acorn.org

Alliance for Better Campaigns
Paul Taylor, Director
1150 17th St NW
Washington DC 20036
(202) 659-1300
www.bettercampaigns.org

Alliance for Democracy
Nick Penniman, National Coordinator
681 Main St
Waltham, MA 02451
(781) 894-1179
thealliancefordemocracy.org

Campaign Reform Project
Cheryl Perrin, Executive Director
50 F St NW, Ste 1198
Washington DC 20001
(202) 628-0610
www.campaignforamerica.org

Center for Public Integrity
Chuck Lewis, Executive Director
910 17th St NW, 7th Floor
Washington DC 20006
(202) 466-1300
www.publicintegrity.org

Center for Responsive Politics
Lawrence Noble, Executive Director
1101 14th St NW, Ste 1030
Washington DC 20005
(202) 857-0044
www.crp.org

Center for Voting and Democracy
Robert Ritchie, Executive Director
PO Box 60037
Washington DC 20039
(301) 270-4616
www.fairvote.org

Common Cause
Eric Swanson, Executive Director
1250 Connecticut Ave NW
Washington DC 20036
(202) 833-1200
www.commoncause.org

Democracy 21
Fred Wertheimer, Executive Director
1825 I St. NW, Suite 400
Washington DC 20006
(202) 429-2008

Initiative and Referendum Institute
M. Dane Waters, President
1825 I St NW, Suite 400
Washington, DC 20006
(202) 429-5539
www.iandrinstitute.org

National Voting Rights Institute
John Bonifaz, Director
1 Bromfield St., 3rd Floor
Boston, MA 02108
(617) 368-9100
www.nvri.org

New England Citizen Action Research Center (NECARC)
David Desiderato, Executive Director
621 Farmington Ave.
Hartford, CT 06105
(860) 231-2410
www.neaction.org

Public Campaign
Nick Nyhart, Executive Director
1320 Nineteenth St, Suite M-1
Washington DC 20036
(202) 293-0222
www.publicampaign.org

Public Citizen
Joan Claybrook, President
1600 20th St NW
Washington DC 20006
(202) 588-1000
www.citizen.org

USPIRG
Gene Karpinski, Director
218 D Street SE
Washington DC 20003
(202) 546-9707
www.uspirg.org

Harry Lonsdale

U.S. Term Limits
Paul Jacob, Executive Director
10 G St NE, Suite 410
Washington DC 20002
(202) 379-3000
www.termlimits.org

Western States Center
Dan Petegorsky, Executive Director
PO Box 40305
Portland, OR 97240
(503) 228-8866
www.westernstatescenter.org

Working Group on Electoral Democracy
Randy Kehler, Executive Director
273 Shelburne Line Rd
Colrain, MA 01340
(413) 624-3836

BIBLIOGRAPHY

Listed below are a few books about politics that I've found particularly enlightening or enjoyable. While most of these books cover a broad range of issues, I've broken the list into several subject areas, for the interested reader.

Corporate Power
Korten, David C., *When Corporations Rule the World*, Kumarian Press, West Hartford, CT, 1995.
Nader, Ralph, *The Ralph Nader Reader*, Seven Stories Press, New York, 2000.

Direct Democracy
Amar, Akhil Reed, and Alan Hirsch, *For the People*, The Free Press, New York, 1998.
Barber, Benjamin R., *A Passion for Democracy*, Princeton University Press, Princeton, N.J., 1998.
Cronin, Thomas E., *Direct Democracy*, Harvard University Press, Cambridge, MA, 1989.
Huffington, Arianna, *How to Overthrow the Government*, Harper Collins, New York, 2000.

Media
Bagdikian, Ben H., *The Media Monopoly*, Beacon Press, Boston, 1997.
Fallows, James, *Breaking the News*, Pantheon Books, New York, 1996.
Frantzich, Stephen, and John Sullivan, *The C-SPAN Revolution*, University of Oklahoma Press, Norman, OK, 1996.
Grossman, Lawrence K., *The Electronic Republic*, Viking, New York, 1995.
Kurtz, Howard, *Media Circus*, Random House, New York, 1993.
McChesney, Robert W., *Rich Media, Poor Democracy*, University of Illinois Press, Urbana, IL, 1999.
Simpson, Alan K., *Right in the Old Gazoo*, William Morrow, New York, 1997.

Money in Politics

Alexander, Herbert E., and Rei Shiratori (Eds.), *Comparative Political Finance Among the Democracies*, Westview Press, Boulder, 1994

Clawson, Dan, Alan Neustadtl, and Mark Weller, *Dollars and Votes*, Temple University Press, Philadelphia, 1998.

Corrado, Anthony, *Campaign Finance Reform*, The Century Foundation Press, New York, 2000.

Etzioni, Amitai, *Capital Corruption*, Transaction Publishers, New Brunswick, NJ 1988.

Greider, William, *Who Will Tell the People*, Simon and Schuster, New York, 1992.

Haddock, Doris, with Dennis Burke, *Granny D. Walking Across America in My Ninetieth Year*, Villard Books, New York, 2001

Jackson, Brooks, *Honest Graft*, Farragut Publishing, Washington, D.C., 1990.

Lewis, Charles, *The Buying of the Congress*, Avon Books, New York, 1998.

Lewis, Charles, *The Buying of the President 2000*, Avon Books, New York, 2000.

Makinson, Larry, *Follow the Money Handbook*, Center for Responsive Politics, Washington, D.C., 1994.

Raskin, Jamin B., and John Bonifaz, *The Wealth Primary*, Center for Responsive Politics, Washington, D.C., 1994.

Stern, Philip M., *Still the Best Congress Money Can Buy*, Regnery Gateway, Washington, D.C.., 1992.

Political Humor

Hightower, Jim, *There's Nothing in the Middle of the Road but Yellow Stripes and Dead Armadillos*, Harper Collins, New York, 1997.

Hightower, Jim, *If the Gods Had Meant Us to Vote They Would Have Given Us Candidates*, Harper Collins, New York, 2000.

Ivins, Molly, *Nothin' but Good Times Ahead*, Random House, New York, 1993.

Ivins, Molly, *You Gotta Dance with Them What Brung You*, Random House, New York, 1998.

Moore, Michael, *Downsize This!*, Crown Publishers, New York, 1996.

Politics

Donaldson, Sam, *Hold On, Mr. President!*, Random House, New York, 1987.
Goodwin, Doris Kearns, *No Ordinary Time*, Simon and Schuster, New York, 1994.
Jamieson, Kathleen Hall, *Dirty Politics*, Oxford University Press, New York, 1992.
Johnson, Haynes, *Sleepwalking Through History*, W.W. Norton, New York, 1991.
Johnson, Haynes, and David S. Broder, *The System*, Little Brown, Boston, 1996.
Matalin, Mary, and James Carville, *All's Fair*, Random House, New York, 1994.
Merriner, James L., and Thomas P. Senter, *Against Long Odds*, Praeger, Westport, CT, 1999.
Peters, Charles, *How Washington Really Works*, Addison-Wesley, Reading, MA, 1980.
Phillips, Kevin, *The Politics of Rich and Poor*, Random House, New York, 1990.
Sanders, Bernie, *Outsider in the House*, Verso, New York, 1997.
Ventura, Jesse, *Do I Stand Alone?*, Pocket Books, New York, 2000.
Zinn, Howard, *The Zinn Reader*, Seven Stories Press, New York, 1997.

Polling

Greenberg, Stanley B., *Middle Class Dreams*, Random House, New York, 1995.
Patterson, James, and Peter Kim, *The Day America Told the Truth*, Prentice Hall, New York, 1991.

Voters Initiative

Broder, David S., *Democracy Derailed*, Harcourt, New York, 2000.
Schmidt, David D., *Citizen Lawmakers*, Temple University Press, Philadelphia, 1989.

Washington Beltway

Barlett, Donald L. and James B. Steele, *America: What Went Wrong?*, Andrews and McMeel, Kansas City, 1992.

Harry Lonsdale

Barlett, Donald L., and James B. Steele, *America: Who Really Pays the Taxes?*, Simon and Schuster, New York, 1994.

CPSIA information can be obtained at www.ICGtesting.com
Printed in the USA
LVOW131318110213

319588LV00001B/45/A